W9-ACW-072

The Great Kite Book

Norman Schmidt

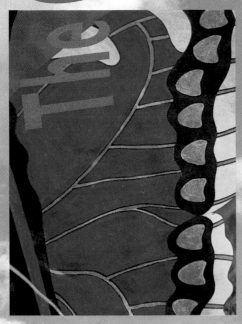

Sterling Publishing Co., Inc. New York

A Sterling/Tamos Book

A Sterling / Tamos Book
© 1997 Norman Schmidt

Sterling Publishing Company, Inc.
387 Park Avenue South, New York, NY 10016

TAMOS Books Inc.
300 Wales Avenue, Winnipeg, MB, Canada R2M 2S9

10   9   8   7   6   5   4   3   2

Distributed in Canada by Sterling Publishing Co., Inc.
c/o Canadian Manda Group, 1 Atlantic Avenue, Suite 105
Toronto, Ontario, Canada M6K 3E7
Distributed in Great Britain and Europe by Cassell PLC
Wellington House, 125 Strand, London WC2R 0BB, England
Distributed in Australia by Capricorn Link (Australia) Pty Ltd.
P.O. Box 6651, Baulkham Hills,
Business Centre, NSW 2153, Australia

Design   Norman Schmidt
Photography   Jerry Grajewski, Custom Images
Illustration of historical kites   Stefan Czernecki

Manufactured in United States of America
All rights reserved

CANADIAN CATALOGING IN PUBLICATION DATA

Schmidt, Norman Jacob, 1947-

The great kite book

"A Sterling/Tamos book."
Includes index.
ISBN 1-895569-36-2 (bound) — ISBN 1-895569-17-6 (pbk.)

1. Kites – Design and construction.   I. Title.

TL759.S35 1996   629.133'32   C96-920147-8

LIBRARY OF CONGRESS
CATALOGING IN PUBLICATION DATA

Schmidt, Norman.
   The great kite book / Norman Schmidt.
       p.   cm.
   "A Sterling/Tamos book."
   Includes index.
   ISBN 1-895569-36-2
   1. Kites   I. Title.
   TL759.S35 1997
   629.133'32 — dc21   96-37195
                              CIP
   HC ISBN 1-895569-36-2
   PB ISBN 1-895569-17-6

Metric measurements have been calculated by
multiplying inches by 2.5 and rounding off
centimeters.

Contents

Kites are universal

Who flew the first kites? It is not known for certain. Probably they were invented quite independently in different parts of the world. Kites first appear in the folklore and ancient writings of oriental cultures. Simple kites consisting of little more than a large tropical leaf on a line, used for fishing, were common in the South Sea islands. On the Chinese mainland people built and elaborately decorated more sophisticated kites that were flown for military and ceremonial purposes.

Although kites were known in early western society and for a time also had ceremonial and military significance, they were eventually regarded as useless objects. Kites in the west gained no religious importance, and increasing urbanization and industrialization prevented the gentle art of kiting from becoming popular. Only during the brief time of experimentation with flight that preceded the invention of the airplane, when kites fired the western imagination with visions of human flight, did kiting become significant. Once airplanes were a reality, however, the popularity of kiting waned. Consequently, many individuals have never experienced the pleasures of home-building these simple airborne wonders. And many people in western cultures still consider kiting an idle waste of time — hence, "go fly a kite," has become a derogatory expression. Other people feel intimidated by kiting, thinking that it is too complicated for them, or they are afraid their kites won't fly because they have no experience with such airborne things.

But times are changing. Industry and technology have not been altogether bad for kite making. They have yielded materials that are ideally suited to this art, and kite enthusiasts are taking advantage of them to create new styles and types having increased maneuverability. This has allowed kite flying to be organized into competitive games, and kiting has become a sport, making kites more visible in many communities around the world. Consequently more people feel inclined to give kiting a try, and kite flying for fun is gaining in popularity once again.

While people fly kites for different reasons, nothing quite matches the satisfaction of getting a kite of one's own research and creation airborne. This is the essence of the art of kiting. It connects the kite flier with the past and gives a sense of participating in something historically significant, knowing that countless numbers of people around the world have engaged in this distinguished activity since time immemorial. Kiting provides mind-soothing satisfaction when that fragile creature, hovering, swooping, swaying back and forth, gently paints the canvas of sky overhead. And a sky full of kites is truly an inspiration to the human spirit.

3

Kite basics

A kite released from the ground flies upward along the arc created by its tether.

WIND SCALE

Light: 1-7 mph (1-11 km/hr)
The wind can just be felt on one's face, leaves are in motion, and smoke drifts.

Gentle: 8-12 mph (12-20 km/hr)
A noticeable breeze. Leaves rustle, small twigs move, and flags flutter.

Moderate: 13-20 mph (21-30 km/hr)
A windy day. Dust is picked up, flags flap, and small branches move.

Strong: over 20 mph (30 km/hr)
Uncomfortably windy. Small trees sway noticeably and debris flies about.

Wind shadow — Air passing over obstacles is turbulent on the downwind side for a distance of about seven times the height of the objects.

Wind

Kites are creatures of the wind. And as there are many kinds of wind, there are many kinds of kites to suit them. It is the sky and the wind, stirring the human imagination, that gave rise to kites in the first place, and it is the wind that determines what kind of kite to fly on any given day. Considering the variables possible in a kite (aspect ratio, lift-to-drag ratio, stability, and angle of attack), flying kites becomes a balancing act in every sense. And learning to "read the wind" is as important to successful kite flying as understanding the principles of flight. Not all kites fly in any kind of wind. On a blustery day, when many people think it must be "good kite weather," chances are the wind is suited only for box kites and aerobatic kites that can tolerate high wind speeds. **Most kites fly in gentle winds with speeds between 8 and 12 miles per hour (12-20 km/hr), when leaves on trees rustle.**

Wind speed also increases with altitude. This is known as the wind gradient. Wind near the ground is slowed by the friction caused by passing over the ground. One might observe the surroundings and think the wind is gentle, but at 1,000 feet (300 m) it might well be strong. Wind gradients can vary considerably. Therefore, even though a kite may not fly at ground level, once at altitude it will fly happily.

Near the ground wind also tends to be turbulent, caused by passing over trees, buildings, and other objects. Besides creating impossible wind conditions, areas with obstacles often present real hazards, such as traffic or overhead wires. Wide open areas are best for kite flying. If obstacles are present, consideration must be given to their "wind shadow," an area of extreme turbulence immediately downwind of an object. **"Wind shadows" cover a distance of at least seven times an object's height.** For example, a 20 foot (6 m) tree has a wind shadow of 140 feet (42 m).

Kite performance

A kite is fundamentally like an airplane on a tether; both fly according to the same aerodynamic principles. Both are heavier than air and must incorporate some means of overcoming the effects of gravity by an upward force utilizing the air flowing across their surfaces. Both must also have a way of remaining stable when airborne.

Three main forces — gravity, lift, and drag — are at work on a kite when in flight. An airplane has a fourth, thrust, to propel it through the air, making its own "wind."

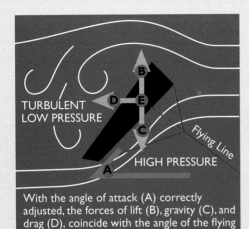

With the angle of attack (A) correctly adjusted, the forces of lift (B), gravity (C), and drag (D), coincide with the angle of the flying line at the center of pressure (E).

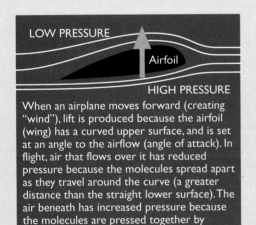

When an airplane moves forward (creating "wind"), lift is produced because the airfoil (wing) has a curved upper surface, and is set at an angle to the airflow (angle of attack). In flight, air that flows over it has reduced pressure because the molecules spread apart as they travel around the curve (a greater distance than the straight lower surface). The air beneath has increased pressure because the molecules are pressed together by striking the lower surface.

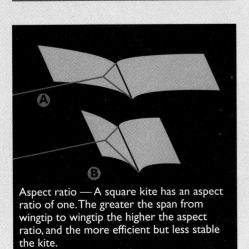

Aspect ratio — A square kite has an aspect ratio of one. The greater the span from wingtip to wingtip the higher the aspect ratio, and the more efficient but less stable the kite.

A kite, like every object, has a center of gravity, the point at which all weight appears concentrated and at which it balances. Likewise it can be said to have a center of lift, the point at which all air pressure against the kite is concentrated, and a center of drag, the point on the kite where all resistant forces are concentrated. In a well balanced kite these forces coincide at a single point, the center of pressure, where the flying line is attached.

Performance and the angle of attack The covering of a kite is its wind-receiving sail. An upward force is created as wind strikes the sail to produce a zone of increased air pressure on its face (facing the person flying it) and a zone of decreased pressure on its backside. To achieve this the kite is set at an angle to the wind so that its leading edge (top) is higher than the tail end, allowing the wind to strike the face at an angle, exerting pressure on it. The sloping of the sail is called the kite's angle of attack. Air is deflected downward, resulting in an opposing upward force being produced — lift. The upward force opposes the force of gravity, making the kite rise into the air.

Not only does air strike the face, but it spills over and around the kite to the backside creating a partial vacuum on the backside, something like a cambered wing (curved airfoil) of an airplane. This lowered pressure sucks the kite upward, adding to the lifting force.

A kite's angle of attack can be much greater than that of an airfoil as found in an airplane wing because of a kite's light weight. A kite can tolerate to be stalled while an airfoil can't. And the air on the backside is more turbulent and separated more from the sail than air over an airfoil. But every kite has an optimum angle of attack, relative to a given wind speed, when the three forces coincide.

Performance and shape Every kite has a relationship of width (span) to length (chord). This is the aspect ratio. A square kite has an aspect ratio of one. A kite that is wider than it is long has a higher aspect ratio. And the higher the aspect ratio is, the more efficient and buoyant the kite becomes, but the kite becomes less stable in the air. On the other hand, a kite with a low aspect ratio is more stable, but less efficient.

Performance and efficiency Not all kites climb as high as others. All lift production has a corresponding penalty of drag because wind striking a kite produces turbulence and friction (induced drag). Any drag-producing parts of a kite (such as decorations and streamers, or a tail) that are not producing lift add to the overall drag, decreasing a kite's efficiency (parasite drag). Therefore every kite, regardless of its weight, has a lift-to-drag ratio, which may be high or low. If a well adjusted kite has a high lift-to-drag ratio, that is, if it is well streamlined, it will climb high along the arc. A kite having a low lift-to-drag ratio, even when well adjusted, will not climb high along its arc.

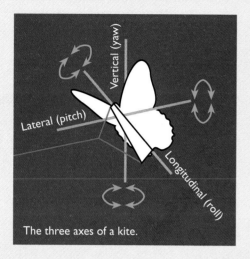

The three axes of a kite.

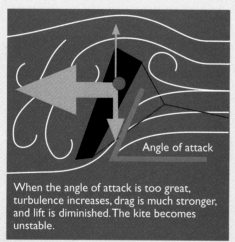

When the angle of attack is too great, turbulence increases, drag is much stronger, and lift is diminished. The kite becomes unstable.

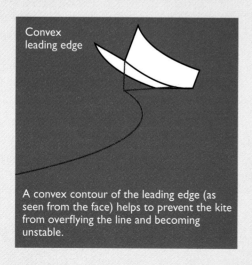

A convex contour of the leading edge (as seen from the face) helps to prevent the kite from overflying the line and becoming unstable.

Kite stability

All kites, regardless of their aspect ratio and efficiency, are relatively unstable and must have a means of stabilizing their flight. A kite tends to roll along its longitudinal axis; yaw along its vertical axis; and pitch along its lateral axis. To counteract, three-axes stability is needed. There are several things that contribute to stability, either by being built into the airframe or added to it. They are, adjusting the angle of attack, giving the kite a dihedral angle, a convex leading edge, a keel, and the addition of a long tail. The most common means of attaining any kind of stability is the addition of a tail. A tail contributes especially to yaw and pitch stability. With the correct angle of attack, even a flat kite can be given enough stability to become airborne with only a tail added. In some kites, strategically placed vents in the sail are yet another means of adding stability. **Most importantly, stabilizers can be used in any combination to maximize their effectiveness.**

Stability and the angle of attack Striking a balance between finding the optimum angle of attack and adjusting the stabilizing devices is not always easy because of the interdependency between a kite's shape, its inherent performance, and its degree of instability, compounded by variations in wind speed.

There is no single overall best angle of attack. Every kite ideally needs to have a different angle of attack for every change in wind speed. If the wind speed increases two things occur. First, the kite begins to slide down its arc because the drag increases, and the angle of attack becomes larger. Second, the kite becomes unstable because the air pressure and accompanying turbulence are so great that they exceed the stabilizer's ability to compensate. Then the kite goes into very tight lateral spins. **If a crash is imminent, to minimize damage, always give a kite plenty of slack line.**

The first remedy is to reduce the angle of attack, allowing more air to spill around the kite, decreasing drag, and allowing the stabilizing system to work. The second is to increase the effectiveness of the stabilizing system itself by adjusting it for the conditions.

Unless some method of making airborne adjustments to the angle of attack or the stabilizer is built in, the best one can do is optimize them for any given flight. **The rule is — low wind speed, high angle of attack; high wind speed, low angle of attack.** Keeping a kite airborne in variable winds is a matter of working the line, increasing and decreasing tension on the line.

Stability and leading-edge contour Sometimes a kite's leading-edge contour causes pitch instability, making a kite climb so that it overflies the line. At low altitudes this can have disastrous results. This kind of pitch instability can be lessened if the leading edge is convex (as seen from the face). This must be built into the airframe of the kite.

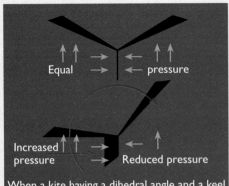

Equal pressure

Increased pressure   Reduced pressure

When a kite having a dihedral angle and a keel is upset by a gust, the pressure increases on the lowered and yawed side. The unequal pressure rights the kite, restoring eqilibrium.

Kites can be stabilized with a variety of tails. Besides their practical purpose, they add decoration.

Stability and the dihedral angle A dihedral angle is the upward slanting of the outer tips of the sail away from the spine. This can be built into the airframe by bowing the spars or fixing the spars at an angle. The kite then has a natural tendency to right itself when upset. Suppose an airborne kite (that has dihedral) dips one wingtip downward. A larger area is exposed to the wind on that side, increasing lift, righting the kite, and restoring equilibrium. This is roll stability.

Stability and a keel An effective way of attaining yaw stability is by giving the kite a keel (a vertical surface). Stability occurs because the airstream flowing past the vertical plane exerts equal pressure on both sides, keeping the kite facing into the wind.

A keel can be built into the airframe. Another kind of keel is formed by filling in (with a material similar to the sail) the triangle made by a normal two-legged bridle.

Sometimes a keel is all that is needed to attain stability over a wide range of wind speeds. If the keel is not sufficiently large, the kite may be stable at lower wind speeds but not when the wind speed increases. Then the addition of a short tail would solve the problem. If the keel is too large the keel will decrease stability because it catches every stray gust of wind, blowing the kite back and forth in the sky.

Stability and a tail By creating drag behind the kite, a tail offsets the tendency for dynamic forces acting on the sail (yaw and pitch) to upset the kite. As the tail sways back and forth, it pulls gently on the kite's spine in the opposite direction. If the tail is of correct length, this back and forth motion is in direct proportion to the upsetting tendency, neutralizing it. If the tail is too long, it will not sway back and forth rhythmically, thereby not stabilizing effectively. And its drag will decrease the overall efficiency of the kite. If the tail is too short, it will be unable to compensate the upsetting tendency of the kite and it will remain unstable in the air.

A tail may consist of a single plain ribbon, a ribbon with a series of tabs attached, a number of ribbons, a large number of ribbons to make a donkey tail, or a series of bows on a string.

As a general rule, for a kite that is primarily dependent on a tail for stability, the tail should be about seven times the length of the spine. But its length must be adjusted according to the wind speed. **The stronger the wind, the longer the tail must be.**

Besides the practical nature of a tail, it also serves as decoration, adding beauty to a kite as it sways back and forth.

Stability and a drogue Sometimes a kite climbs so rapidly, either because it is very buoyant or the wind decreases, that it overflies the line, rising along its arc past the zenith. This greatly reduces the angle of attack, allowing the line to go slack, and the kite goes into a series of large lateral loops. If this cannot be corrected by changing the angle of attack or lengthening the tail, adding a drogue may help.

A drogue is simply a short conical fabric tube with the large end facing into the wind, something like a short windsock or narrow parachute. A shroud fastens it to a line, which is then attached to the kite. Unlike a tail, a drogue does not create drag along its length, but concentrates it within the cone. The result is not compensatory undulation in the airstream, but a lever effect. A drogue pulls its line taut, and the longer the line the greater the stabilizing effect.

A variation on the drogue is the more decorative spinner. The spinner's cone consists of a number of fabric triangles collected at a central point. Instead of air escaping from a single small opening at the end, it escapes between the triangles, setting the device spinning. When a number of ribbons are attached, it becomes quite a spectacle in the air.

Bridling a kite

The bridle is the loop of string attached to the kite's spine, running front to back. A good knot to use for this is an anchor hitch. To the bridle is attached the flying line (tether) at a location called the towing point, dividing the bridle into two legs. The positioning of the towing point is very important because it determines the angle of attack that a kite can assume relative to the flying line. Moving the towing point changes the angle of attack. The correct positioning of the towing point on the bridle is important if the maximum performance of a kite is to be realized. If the towing point is in the wrong place, even the best of kites will not get airborne successfully.

There is no hard and fast rule about how long the loop of the bridle line should be. **Generally, the bridle should be of sufficient length so that the towing point is away from the spine by a distance of at least half a spine length.**

The approximate place along the bridle at which the towing point will fall can be ascertained quite easily before a kite is flown, but the precise point can only be determined in the field. Lay the kite on its back and, draping the bridle loop over one finger, lift the kite slightly off the ground. By sliding the string, slant the kite so that the tail end of the spine touches the ground and the front is raised. The angle thus formed between the spine and the ground should be between 20° and 30°. The point at which the string then drapes over the finger is the approximate towing point. Mark this point using a felt pen and attach a towing ring to the bridle line at this point, using a lark's head hitch.

Fine tuning the towing point must be done relative to the wind speed at any given time. **To increase the angle of attack, move the towing ring toward the tail end of the bridle line. To decrease the angle of attack, move it forward.**

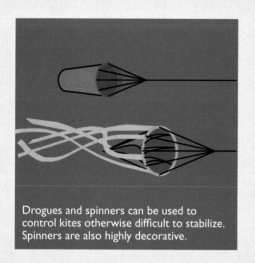

Drogues and spinners can be used to control kites otherwise difficult to stabilize. Spinners are also highly decorative.

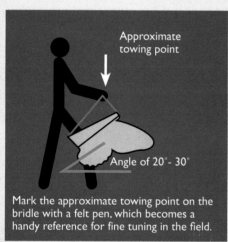

Approximate towing point

Angle of 20° - 30°

Mark the approximate towing point on the bridle with a felt pen, which becomes a handy reference for fine tuning in the field.

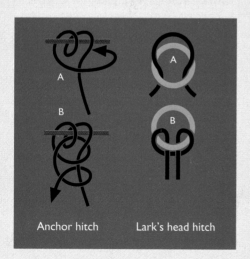

A

B

A

B

Anchor hitch   Lark's head hitch

There are some kites that need a bridle having more than just two legs. For example, kites with fragile frames, or those without frames like limp canopy type kites. In the latter the bridle has so many legs that it is called a shroud. Then the bridle serves not just as an attachment for the flying line, but also as a support for the wind-receiving sail.

Flying line

The type of flying line used also has a bearing on performance. As a kite gains altitude, and an increasing amount of line is let out, the weight the kite must bear increases. Not only the actual weight of the string is involved, but also the length of line: as it increases, so does the drag of the wind striking the line. At a certain point the kite is no longer able to climb, the line just sags more. To minimize this drag, use the lightest, thinnest, and smoothest line that a kite in any particular wind can use without breaking the string.

Launching kites

Given that all adjustments of bridle and stabilizers have been balanced and conditions are perfect, a kite presented to the wind should fly directly from one's hand, rising skyward effortlessly along its arc, moving back and forth gently in the currents of air. If there is not quite enough wind near the ground, pumping the line as it rises through the wind gradient may help, until the kite reaches stronger wind higher up.

Alternately a "high start" can be tried. This requires two people. One person holds the line and another the kite. Line is let out as one person walks downwind with the kite to a distance of at least 100 feet (30 m), perhaps more. With the line taut, the kite is released. The kite operator immediately applies additional pressure to the line by reeling it in, pumping the line, walking backwards, or some combination of these. However, a close watch must be kept on the kite, and just the right amount of pressure applied. (Running with a kite is not a good idea, because not enough attention can be paid to the kite's behavior.)

It is essential that the stabilizing system used is given a chance to take immediate effect, otherwise an upset will occur. Therefore a tail should not be held bunched up, but allowed to fly freely from the ground up. And not too much pressure should be exerted on the line by the operator.

When the kite achieves some altitude and a sufficiently strong wind is found, the high start is successful if the kite maintains the altitude. But if no stronger wind is found aloft the kite will settle back down to the ground. The operator should give it free line as it descends. Another high start can then be tried, using a longer line to gain more altitude.

The kite on the left has a thin smooth line. The one on the right has a heavy coarse line. Although the kites are identical, the heavy line increases drag, making the line sag.

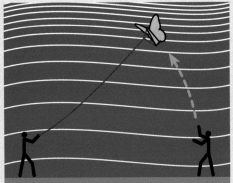

For a high start, the person on the left puts tension on the line as the kite is released and climbs through the wind gradient. If sufficient wind is found, the kite will stay aloft.

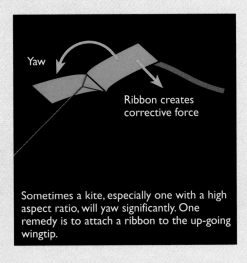

Yaw

Ribbon creates corrective force

Sometimes a kite, especially one with a high aspect ratio, will yaw significantly. One remedy is to attach a ribbon to the up-going wingtip.

About the kites in this book

Ever since the first kites were built materials and methods have been changing. In the Orient these changes were realized in a slow evolution of styles unique to various locations. These styles became established as traditions that were passed down from generation to generation. Kite art became highly refined, practiced by master craftsmen.

Traditional oriental kites utilize a semi-rigid frame made from bamboo, wood, and string, covered with paper or fabric bearing colorful images. The westernization of kites coincided with increasing technological innovation between the eighteenth and twentieth centuries, immediatley preceding the invention of the airplane. Since there were no traditional biases, new ideas about materials and methods emerged freely. On the one hand innovation led to successful airplanes, and on the other it led to different kinds of kites.

One new twentieth-century material is Tyvek™ (DuPont), made from spunbonded polyethylene. It is made in a sheet form that resembles paper, as well as a softer cloth-like form. The sheet form does not stretch, can be cut without fraying, does not tear easily, and can be sewn, glued, and colored. It is distributed by paper merchants and can be obtained readily from any printing shop.

The kites in this book take advantage of sheet form Tyvek because of its inherent qualities. All the kites follow a similar method of construction which is based on Tyvek's strength and its resistance to stretching. All the kites are constructed with no perimeter frame. The main frame is attached directly to the Tyvek, leaving the entire kite flexible. Building such a "flex-frame" kite requires careful positioning of the frame so that it gives support to the sail in a way that allows the natural pressure of the wind against the sail to give it aerodynamic form. A main spreader strut gives the kite a fixed dihedral angle at the front spars. The rear spars may have a secondary strut. The entire frame flexes, giving shape to the sail, as determined by the wind pressure. A built-in keel gives stability.

The kites have a relatively shallow angle of attack, exerting only a light pressure on the bridle and flying line. A light cotton string is sufficient for both.

Applying this "flex-frame" principle, a wide variety of airworthy kites has been included here, resembling various flying creatures. They can be built using non-specialized tools and techniques simple enough for anyone to master. Once the principle is understood, it can be applied to kites resembling many other creatures or objects,

NOTE: Experimentation is possible with all of the kites. For example, you might change the dihedral angle by lengthening or shortening the spreader struts. Or you could try building a kite without a keel to discover what effect this might have. And of course different tails can always be tried.

limited only by the builder's imagination. It is hoped that these kites will inspire you to attempt your own creations.*

The following list outlines the things needed to build the kites in this book.

Tyvek ™ (DuPont)
Standard sheet size — 36 in x 30 in (90 cm x 75 cm).
Thickness — .0056 calliper.
Tyvek is distributed by paper merchants and is available from any local printing shop.

Hardwood dowels
Standard sizes — ranging from 1/8 in (3 mm) diameter
to 1/4 in (6 mm).
Hardwood dowels are available at hardware stores or lumberyards.

Flexible polyethylene tubing
Polyethylene tubing is available in various degrees of rigidity. Rigid tubing is required. Inside diameters must match the dowels — from 1/8 in (3 mm) to 1/4 in (6 mm).
Polyethylene tubing is available from hardware stores, automotive parts suppliers, or home wine-making shops.

String, towing rings, and swivel hooks
Light cotton string or heavy sewing thread for the bridle and flying line. Split rings or drink can pull-tabs for towing rings, and fishing line swivels. A suitable line reel is also needed.

Shop equipment
Shop equipment such as ruler, pencil, craft knife, scissors, masking tape, white craft glue (the kind that remains flexible when dry), small saw, and sandpaper are required for construction.

For decorating Tyvek use transparent acrylics, such as Createx™ (designed for use in airbrushes). These can also be applied by brush. Giant felt markers can also be used with success. Especially useful are refillable ones such as Pantone Tria™.

All the kites in this book use similar construction techniques: lay out the pattern on a Tyvek sheet, cut out the shape of the kite, add color, and fasten the frame to the sheet. (Detailed instructions are given on the following pages.)

Shown above are the materials for one kite (the Bat) – Tyvek sheeting for the sail, dowels cut to size for the frame, fastening tabs cut to size from scrap Tyvek, joiners cut from polyethylene tubing, string for the bridle, and a split ring for the towing ring.

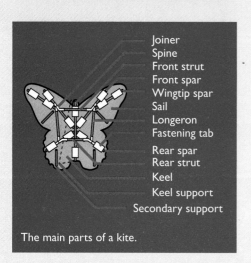

Joiner
Spine
Front strut
Front spar
Wingtip spar
Sail
Longeron
Fastening tab

Rear spar
Rear strut
Keel
Keel support
Secondary support

The main parts of a kite.

* See also Ito, Dr. Toshio, and Hirotsugu Komura. *Kites: The Science and the Wonder*. Japan Publications, Inc., Tokyo, 1983.

Instructions

These general instructions can be followed to make all the kites in this book

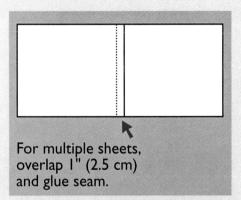

For multiple sheets, overlap 1" (2.5 cm) and glue seam.

Step 1

Some of the kites require one whole sheet of Tyvek (standard sheet size of 36 in x 30 in – 90 cm x 75 cm), others need only part of a sheet, and some more than one. For kites made from a single sheet, lay sheet flat in a horizontal direction. For large kites requiring more than one sheet, begin by assembling multiple sheets as needed, then proceed as though it were a single sheet. Build the kites on a suitable flat surface.

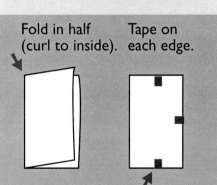

Fold in half (curl to inside).   Tape on each edge.

Step 2

Fold sheet in half so that left edge meets right edge. Tape edges so that the folded sheet remains aligned. The outer sides of the folded sheet will become the kite's face. (Note: Tyvek has a natural tendency to curl. Make sure that when the sheet is folded, the curl is toward the inside so that when the kite is finished, the convex side of the curl is on the face.)

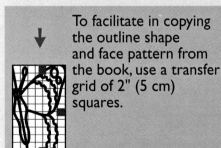

To facilitate in copying the outline shape and face pattern from the book, use a transfer grid of 2" (5 cm) squares.

Step 3

Using the grid method, transfer the kite's outline shape and its decoration pattern from the book onto the folded Tyvek sheet. This will become the **righthand** side of the kite's face. Take note of the area that will become the kite's keel. (Note: First draw lines lightly in pencil. Then darken using felt marker. Finally, to get the pattern onto the other side of the kite, trace the lines showing through the sheets onto the opposite (**lefthand**) side using a window or a lightbox to aid in seeing the lines.

Lay the kite flat facedown. Measure and draw lines for the keel and frame positions.

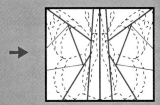

Step 4

Remove tape from edges and unfold sheet. Lay sheet flat facedown. On the backside, measure and draw lines for the keel folds, the main frame positions, and the secondary supports, as shown in the book for each particular kite.

With sheet folded and edges taped, cut out the kite's outline shape.

Step 5

Refold and tape edges as before. Using either a craft knife or a pair of scissors, cut out the outline shape of the kite.

Paint the face of the kite.

Step 6

Unfold and lay the kite flat faceside up. Add color to the face of the sail, either following the color scheme shown or inventing your own.

b) Glue seam.

Step 7

Fold along drawn lines (step 4) to make the keel. Glue the seam. Add one reinforcement tab at the point where the front spars meet the seam, and one where the rear spars meet the seam.

a) Fold to make keel. c) Add tabs.

Cut dowels to lengths needed.

← Bevel edges. Mark concave.

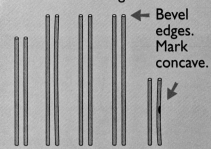

Step 8

With the exception of the longerons, cut all the wood dowel frame pieces to the lengths given for each particular kite. Bevel the edges. (Note: Wood dowels have a natural tendency to bow. Make a mark on the concave side of each of the frame pieces for later reference.)

To make frame joiners, cut polyethylene tubing to the length needed and cut a notch in the middle.

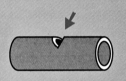

Step 9

Cut polyethylene tubing into short lengths for the frame joiners. Cut a notch in the middle of each piece to complete joiner.

Attach spine dowel over keel seam.

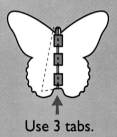

Use 3 tabs.

Step 10

Using three tabs, glue the spine into position along the keel seam to the backside of the sail. (Note: When attached, the concave side of the bow should be facing away from the sail.)

Measure and mark spars for joiner positions.

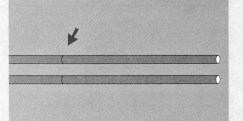

Step 11

On the front and rear spars, measure and mark the positions for the frame joiners. (Note: For easier reference, make the mark as a line drawn completely around the dowel's circumference.)

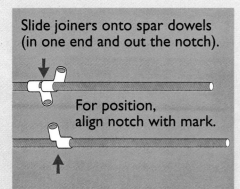

Slide joiners onto spar dowels (in one end and out the notch).

For position, align notch with mark.

Step 12

Slide the frame joiners onto the front and rear spar dowels to the correct positions. For all kites, the front spars need two joiners each, one for the longerons and one for the spreader strut. For some kites, the rear spars need only one for the longerons. Others require two on both the front and rear spars because the kites need a spreader strut at both front and rear spars. (See frame layout for each particular kite.)

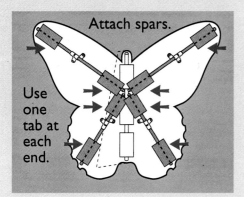

Attach spars.

Use one tab at each end.

Step 13

Using the lines drawn in step 4 as guides, fasten the front and rear main spars to the sail using one tab at each end. (Note: When the spars are attached to the sail, the concave bowing should be facing away from the sail. Achieving this will require rotating the joiners on the dowels before attaching them to the sail.)

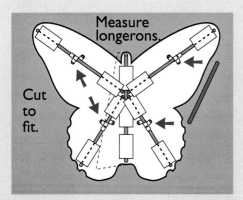

Measure longerons.

Cut to fit.

Step 14

Measure between the front and rear spar frame joiners to determine the length of the longerons. Cut the longerons and bevel edges. (If the spars have been attached symmetrically, the lefthand and righthand measurements should be the same.)

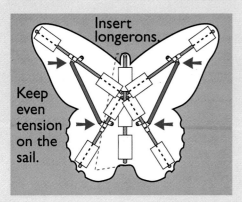

Insert longerons.

Keep even tension on the sail.

Step 15

Once the glue on the tabs for the spars has set, on each side, slide one end of the longeron into the open end of the frame joiner on the rear spar. Then carefully ease the other end into the joiner on the front spar. Make sure that there is even tension on the sail.

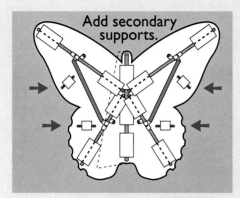

Add secondary supports.

Step 16

Most kites need secondary supports to stiffen the sail. Some kites also require two front spars – main spars and wing spars – on each side (see frame layout for each particular kite). Using the lines drawn in step 4 as guides, fasten the wing spars and secondary supports to the sail.

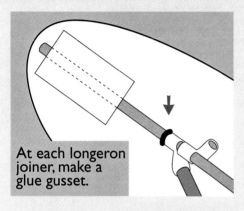

At each longeron joiner, make a glue gusset.

Step 17

Put a small amount of glue at each outside end of the frame joiners, making a gusset of glue to keep the joiners in place. This completes the main frame.

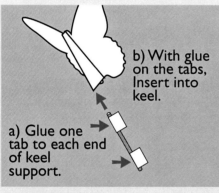

b) With glue on the tabs, Insert into keel.

a) Glue one tab to each end of keel support.

Step 18

Fasten a tab to each end of the keel support dowel. (Also see next step.) The tabs are used to glue the support into the keel and give extra strength for the bridle attachments. With glue on the tabs, slide dowel into the keel and press into place. (Note: When finished, the concave side of the bow should be facing the back.)

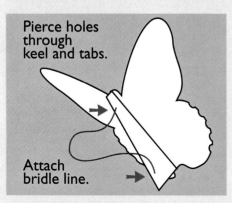

Pierce holes through keel and tabs.

Attach bridle line.

Step 19

At each tab, pierce a hole through the keel and the tab. For the exact location of bridle attachments, see the frame layout for each kite. Using these holes as the attachment points for the kite bridle, tie the bridle line to the keel support dowel using an anchor hitch (see p. 8).

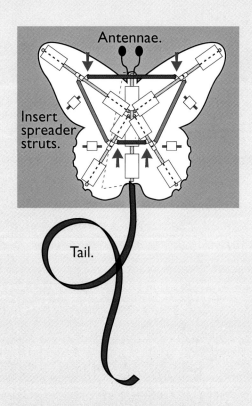

Antennae.

Insert
spreader
struts.

Tail.

Step 20

To complete the kite, insert each end of the spreader strut or struts into the remaining frame joiners on the front spars (or front and rear spars as needed).

If a tail is required, tie it to the end of the spine. Crepe paper decorating ribbon makes a good tail. A strip of Tyvek can also be used. (Note: The antennae on butterflies are optional. If they are included, stiffen them with wire.)

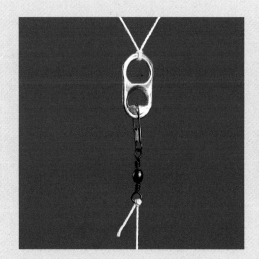

Above, a drink can pull-tab used as a towing ring and a fishing line swivel hook used to attach the flying line.

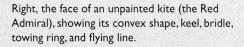

Right, the face of an unpainted kite (the Red Admiral), showing its convex shape, keel, bridle, towing ring, and flying line.

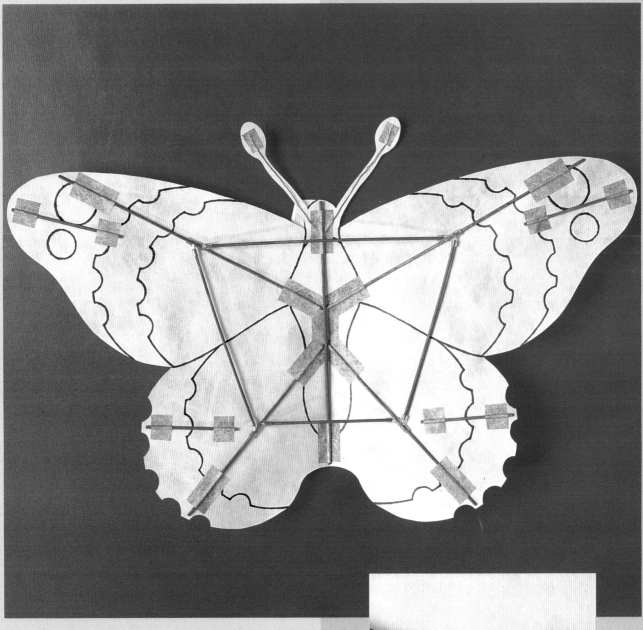

Above, the frame of a kite (the Red Admiral), showing the dowels, joiners, and tabs.

Right, the polyethylene frame joiners in place. (Shown is the left front spar, longeron, and strut connection.)

Great Kites to Build

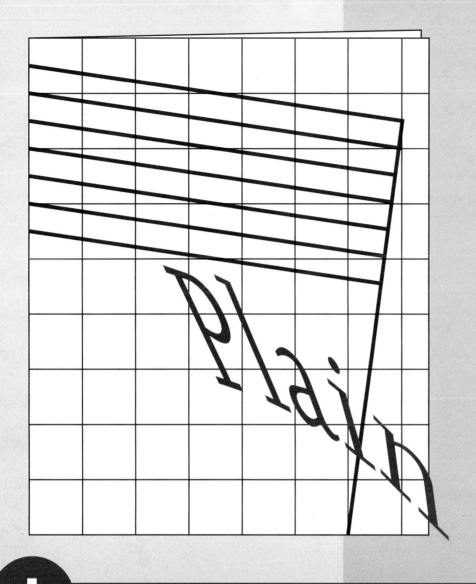

Plain Kite

This kite requires a Tyvek sheet size of
30 in x 18 in (75 cm x 45 cm).

Shown here is the sheet folded in half to
15 in x 18 in (37.5 cm x 45 cm), displaying the
righthand side of the kite's face pattern. A 2 inch
(5 cm) grid is used to facilitate in transferring the
pattern onto the Tyvek sheet (see p 12).

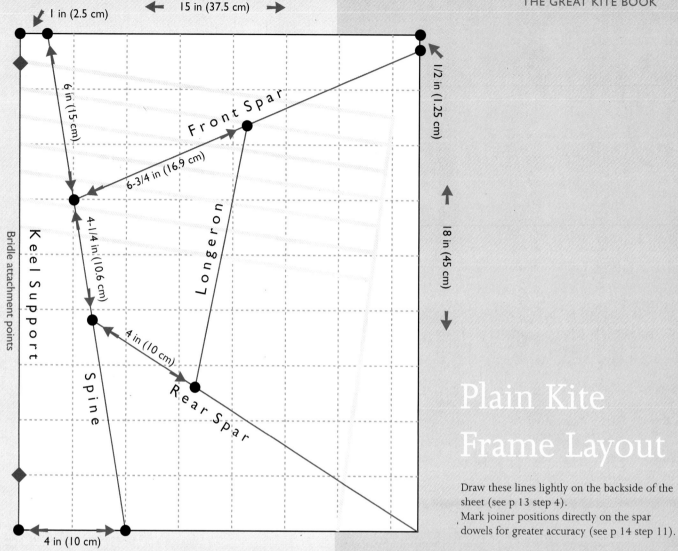

Plain Kite Frame Layout

Draw these lines lightly on the backside of the sheet (see p 13 step 4).
Mark joiner positions directly on the spar dowels for greater accuracy (see p 14 step 11).

Description of framing materials

Spine: 1 wood dowel – 1/8 in x 18 in (.3 cm x 37.5 cm)
Keel support: 1 wood dowel – 1/8 in x 18 in (.3 cm x 37.5 cm)
Front spars: 2 wood dowels – 1/8 in x 13-1/2 in (.3 cm x 33.8 cm)
Wingtip spars: none
Rear spars: 2 wood dowels – 1/8 in x 13-1/2 in (.3 cm x 33.8 cm)
Longerons: 2 wood dowels – measure and cut to fit, approximately 9 in (22.5 cm)
Front spreader strut: 1 wood dowel – 1/8 in x 11-1/4 in (.3 cm x 28 cm)
Rear spreader strut: 1 wood dowel – 1/8 in x 5 in (.3 cm x 12.5 cm)
Polyethylene joiners: 8 pieces – 1/8 in (.3 cm) ID, x 3/4 in (2 cm), notched in the middle
Secondary supports: none
Fastening tabs: about 13 pieces cut from scrap Tyvek, approximately 1-1/4 x 2 in (3 cm x 5 cm)

From mythical origins to high technology

Probably as early as 1000 B.C. ancient Chinese flew sophisticated bamboo and silk kites. This highly developed tool-using people had all the right ingredients to make kiting possible — lightweight bamboo plants for frames, silkworm culture for cloth and string, and ingenious craftsmanship.

Kites continued to gain cultural status. Legends, both domestic and military, contributed to the kite's importance. They described how soldiers were lofted to spy on enemy encampments and of kites mediating with spirits, believed to inhabit the sky.

By the first century A.D. the Chinese discovered how to make a delicate paper from the inner bark of the mulberry tree, the leaves of which were the main diet of silkworms. This paper came to replace silk as the primary writing material and was used for kites as well. The first kites were probably rectangular, but later many exotic kites were made in the shapes of birds, insects, animals, imaginary creatures, and even people. The invention of paper played a major role in popularizing the art of kite making. An annual Chinese Kite Day was celebrated in many regions and a variety of local kite traditions arose.

With the coming of the industrialized age and widespread urbanization, the art of kiting has diminished in China. During Mao Tse Tung's Cultural Revolution of the 1960s, kite flying was outlawed and became an underground activity. It has since regained favor and today is considered an important part of the Chinese cultural heritage.

During the Tang Dynasty (618 A.D.—907 A.D.), the traditions of kiting were carried by wandering Buddhist monks from ancient China across Indo-China to the islands of Japan.

Of kites and chrysanthemums

The myth of Haun Ching tells how a Chinese peasant farmer visited a local fortune-teller, who predicted calamity for the man and his family on the ninth day of the ninth month. These ancient people believed that the sky was the home of spirits. He said to avert disaster, the man should take his family to the distant hills on that day. There they were to drink wine made from chrysanthemum flowers and fly kites that could reach the spirit world in the sky and carry away their misfortunes.

When the family returned to their village that evening, they found all the barnyard animals dead. Since then, on the anniversary of their escape from death, the family and the villagers went to the hills to fly kites. Eventually people believed that an entire year's misfortunes could be averted by flying kites on that day.

This is the origin of Chinese Kite Day, an ancient festival that has been celebrated widely across the entire country.

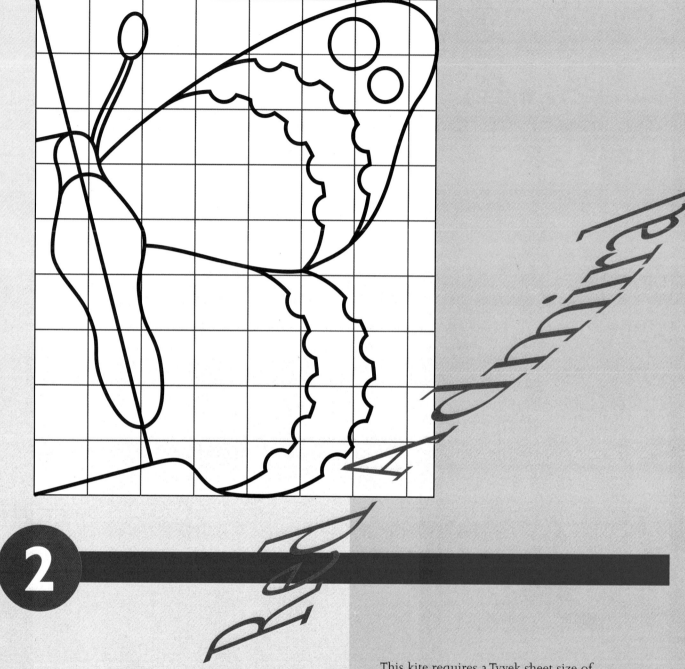

2

This kite requires a Tyvek sheet size of
30 in x 18 in (75 cm x 45 cm).

Shown here is the sheet folded in half to
15 in x 18 in (37.5 cm x 45 cm), displaying the
righthand side of the kite's face pattern. A 2 inch
(5 cm) grid is used to facilitate in transferring the
pattern onto the Tyvek sheet (see p 12).

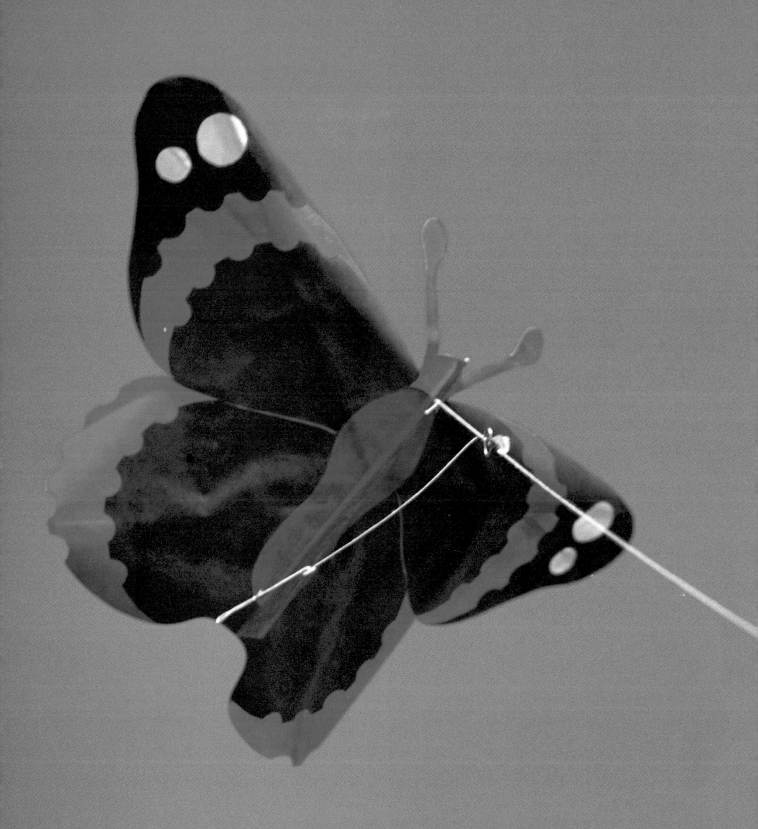

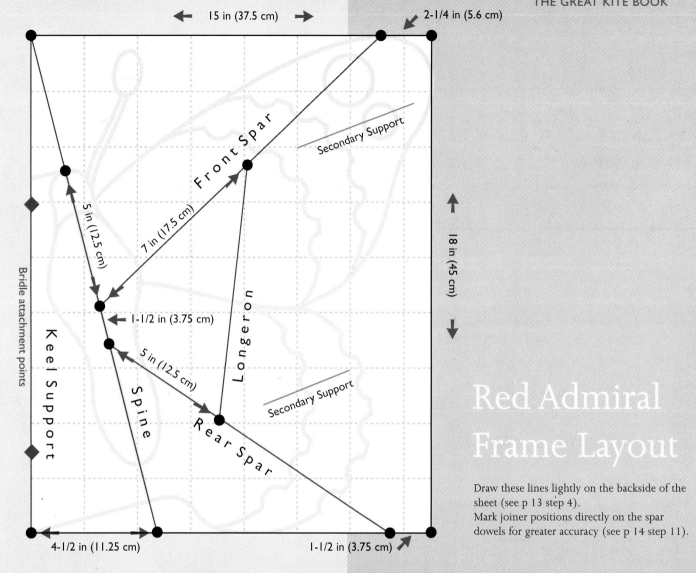

Red Admiral Frame Layout

Draw these lines lightly on the backside of the sheet (see p 13 step 4).
Mark joiner positions directly on the spar dowels for greater accuracy (see p 14 step 11).

Description of framing materials

Spine: 1 wood dowel – 1/8 in x 12-1/4 in (.3 cm x 30.6 cm)

Keel support: 1 wood dowel – 1/8 in x 13 in (.3 cm x 32.5 cm)

Front spars: 2 wood dowels – 1/8 in x 13-1/2 in (.3 cm x 33.8 cm)

Wingtip spars: none

Rear spars: 2 wood dowels – 1/8 in x 10 in (.3 cm x 25 cm)

Longerons: 2 wood dowels – measure and cut to fit, approximately 8-1/2 in (21.3 cm)

Front spreader strut: 1 wood dowel – 1/8 in x 11 in (.3 cm x 27.5 cm)

Rear spreader strut: 1 wood dowel – 1/8 in x 6 in (.3 cm x 15 cm)

Polyethylene joiners: 8 pieces – 1/8 in (.3 cm) ID, x 3/4 in (2 cm), notched in the middle

Secondary supports: 1/8 in wood dowels – 4 short pieces

Fastening tabs: about 18 pieces cut from scrap Tyvek, approximately 1-1/4 x 2 in (3 cm x 5 cm)

In Japan, kites first became an important part of Buddhist religious ritual, and were flown only by the aristocracy. A particular ceremony involved tying unthreshed rice to a kite, flying it over growing crops, intending to invoke the gods to provide an abundant rice harvest.

Traditional Chinese kites.

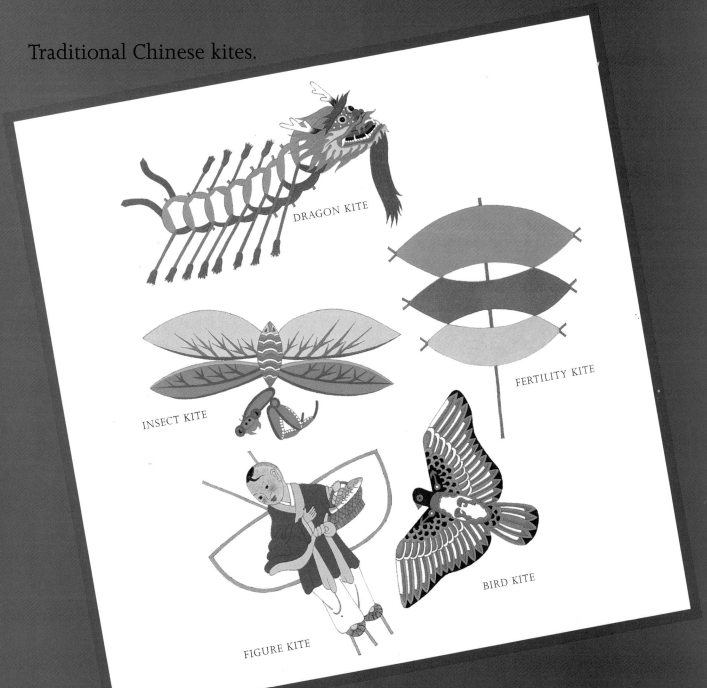

DRAGON KITE

FERTILITY KITE

INSECT KITE

BIRD KITE

FIGURE KITE

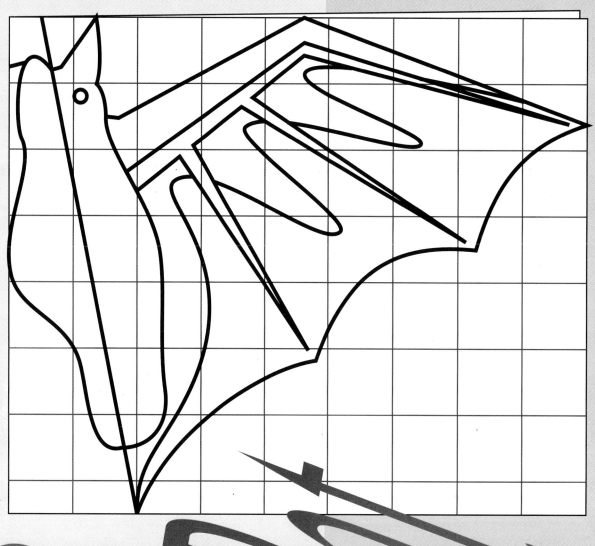

This kite requires a Tyvek sheet size of
36 in x 15 in (90 cm x 37.5 cm).

Shown here is the sheet folded in half to
18 in x 15 in (45 cm x 37.5 cm), displaying the
righthand side of the kite's face pattern. A 2 inch
(5 cm) grid is used to facilitate in transferring the
pattern onto the Tyvek sheet (see p 12).

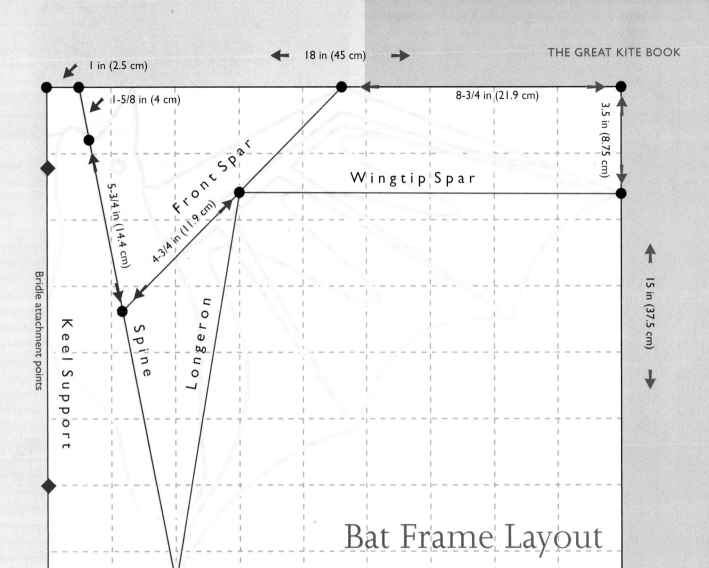

Bat Frame Layout

Draw these lines lightly on the backside of the sheet (see p 13 step 4).
Mark joiner positions directly on the spar dowels for greater accuracy (see p 14 step 11).

Description of framing materials

Spine: 1 wood dowel – 1/8 in x 14 in (.3 cm x 35 cm)

Keel support: 1 wood dowel – 1/8 in x 13-1/2 in (.3 cm x 33.8 cm)

Front spars: 2 wood dowels – 1/8 in x 9-1/2 in (.3 cm x 23.8 cm)

Wingtip spars: 2 wood dowels – 1/8 in x 11 in (.3 cm x 27.5 cm)

Rear spars: none

Longerons: 2 wood dowels – measure and cut to fit, approximately 9-1/2 in (23.8 cm)

Front spreader strut: 1 wood dowel – 1/8 in x 6-3/4 in (.3 cm x 16.9 cm)

Rear spreader strut: none

Polyethylene joiners: 4 pieces – 1/8 in (.3 cm) ID, x 3/4 in (2 cm), notched in the middle

Secondary supports: none

Fastening tabs: about 9 pieces cut from scrap Tyvek, approximately 1-1/4 x 2 in (3 cm x 5 cm)

By the Edo period (1603–1868) kites became universally popular in Japan. They bore likenesses of famous personalities of Japanese kabuki theater and heroes from the art of wood block printing. To celebrate the reconstruction of the Rengiji Temple in 1692, giant kites such as the oval wan-wan were flown. This was the largest kite ever built, about 65 feet (20 m) in diameter and weighing about 5,500 pounds (2,500 kg). It took up to 200 strong men to fly it. Sometimes, if the wind did not subside overnight, it remained airborne for days because it was impossible to haul down.

Another event involving giant kites has become a Japanese tradition. In 1737 a canal that divides the Shirone district into eastern and western regions was rebuilt after it had collapsed during a flood. In celebration, Mizoguchi, lord of the local castle, gave the village of East Shirone a giant kite. Unfortunately it accidentally crashed in West Shirone causing widespread damage to rice crops. The farmers wanted to fight. Instead of war with weapons, Mizoguchi organized a kite battle. To this day, every June, many teams consisting of about fifty participants each, from both East and West Shirone, hold a five-day mock battle with giant o-dako (rectangular) and rokkaku (hexagonal) kites to celebrate the event. Many hundreds of kites are involved, the sky becoming a tangle of lines. After the kites themselves have been destroyed, the event ends with spectators joining the team members in a gigantic tug-of-war with the mass of kite lines. The side having the most line is declared the winner.

Victory by kite

During the bloody territorial battles of ancient China, the warlord Liu Pang was attempting to overthrow the existing rule of Huan Theng who seemed certain to lose.

Legend has it that on the very day that defeat seemed imminent, a gust of wind blew Huan Theng's hat from his head, giving him an idea. He had each of his men build a kite fitted with a noise maker (probably a buzzer made by attaching bamboo strips to a taut string).

After dark the soldiers released the kites on the night wind high above the heads of Liu Pang's sleeping men. For those people the sky was the home of spirits. Being wakened out of a dead sleep by shrieking and wailing overhead, the bewildered soldiers thought they were being attacked by a horde of demons. Terrified, they fled, giving Huan Theng the victory.

4

Bumble Bee

This kite requires a Tyvek sheet size of
30 in x 18 in (75 cm x 45 cm).

Shown here is the sheet folded in half to
15 in x 18 in (37.5 cm x 45 cm), displaying the
righthand side of the kite's face pattern. A 2 inch
(5 cm) grid is used to facilitate in transferring the
pattern onto the Tyvek sheet (see p 12).

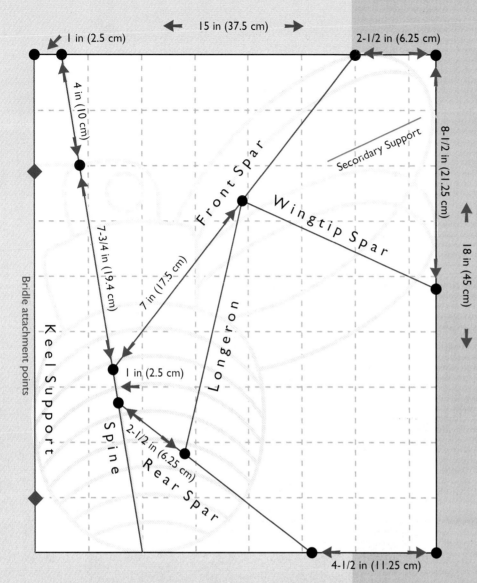

15 in (37.5 cm)

1 in (2.5 cm)

2-1/2 in (6.25 cm)

4 in (10 cm)

8-1/2 in (21.25 cm)

Secondary Support

Front Spar

Wingtip Spar

18 in (45 cm)

Bridle attachment points

7-3/4 in (19.4 cm)

7 in (17.5 cm)

Keel Support

Longeron

1 in (2.5 cm)

Spine

2-1/2 in (6.25 cm)

Rear Spar

4-1/2 in (11.25 cm)

Bumble Bee Frame Layout

Draw these lines lightly on the backside of the sheet (see p 13 step 4).
Mark joiner positions directly on the spar dowels for greater accuracy (see p 14 step 11).

Description of framing materials

Spine: 1 wood dowel – 1/8 in x 14 in (.3 cm x 35 cm)

Keel support: 1 wood dowel – 1/8 in x 14 in (.3 cm x 35 cm)

Front spars: 2 wood dowels – 1/8 in x 14 in (.3 cm x 35 cm)

Wingtip spars: 2 wood dowels – 1/8 in x 7 in (.3 cm x 17.5 cm)

Rear spars: 2 wood dowels – 1/8 in x 5 in (.3 cm x 12.5 cm)

Longerons: 2 wood dowels – measure and cut to fit, approximately 7-1/2 in (18.8 cm)

Front spreader strut: 1 wood dowel – 1/8 in x 8-1/2 in (.3 cm x 21.3 cm)

Rear spreader strut: none

Polyethylene joiners: 6 pieces – 1/8 in (.3 cm) ID, x 3/4 in (2 cm), notched in the middle

Secondary supports: 1/8 in wood dowels – 2 short pieces

Fastening tabs: about 11 pieces cut from scrap Tyvek, approximately 1-1/4 x 2 in (3 cm x 5 cm)

Smaller, more maneuverable "fighting" kites were introduced to Japan in the Edo period by traders from the Dutch East Indies through the port city of Nagasaki. They are called Nagasaki hata kites and still bear the colors of the Dutch flag.

Another festival in Japan involving kites is Children's Day, celebrated on the fifth day of the fifth month. Many kites are flown to celebrate births in the preceding twelve months. In honor of their newborn children, families also fly highly decorative and brightly colored windsocks in the shape of carp, a fish prized in Japan. Carp windsocks are usually set on a bamboo pole in the family garden, but sometimes they are attached to kite lines and flown high in the sky. As the windsocks fill with air and begin to move, they resemble carp swimming against a strong current. This is a sign of strength and vigor, symbolic of the hoped-for progress in the children's lives.

Traveling samuri warriors and traders carried Edo kites to the outlying regions of the country, where they became the basis for the development of distinctive regional kite styles, made by master builders. Sadly, the Japanese art of kiting is in decline. The aging kite makers who learned the art from their elders are no longer passing it along to the next generation.

The wandering monks who brought kites to ancient Japan also brought them to other asiatic regions. Koreans became avid kite flyers and also developed kiting customs intended to ensure good fortune for their children. In Malaysia, the tradition of flying kites to curry favor from the spirits to provide a rich harvest was also practiced. At first kites of simple design were involved, but in time more highly decorated kites were constructed to warrant the bestowing of greater favors. Kites were made from richly embellished and brightly colored glazed tissue paper with floral

The great escape

In ancient Japan the Shogun Minamoto no Tametomo of the Genji clan, and his young son, were exiled to the remote island of Hachijo by a rival clan. To escape the desolate place, the father built a large kite. When the wind was favorable, his son climbed aboard and was carried safely back to the mainland where he built a huge bonfire to signal to his father that he had arrived safely and was on his way to gather support for their clan. Since that time the traditional Hachijo kite has borne the likeness of Tametomo upon its sail.

Barn Swallow

5

This kite requires a Tyvek sheet size of
36 in x 15 in (90 cm x 37.5 cm).

Shown here is the sheet folded in half to
18 in x 15 in (45 cm x 37.5 cm), displaying the
righthand side of the kite's face pattern. A 2 inch
(5 cm) grid is used to facilitate in transferring the
pattern onto the Tyvek sheet (see p 12).

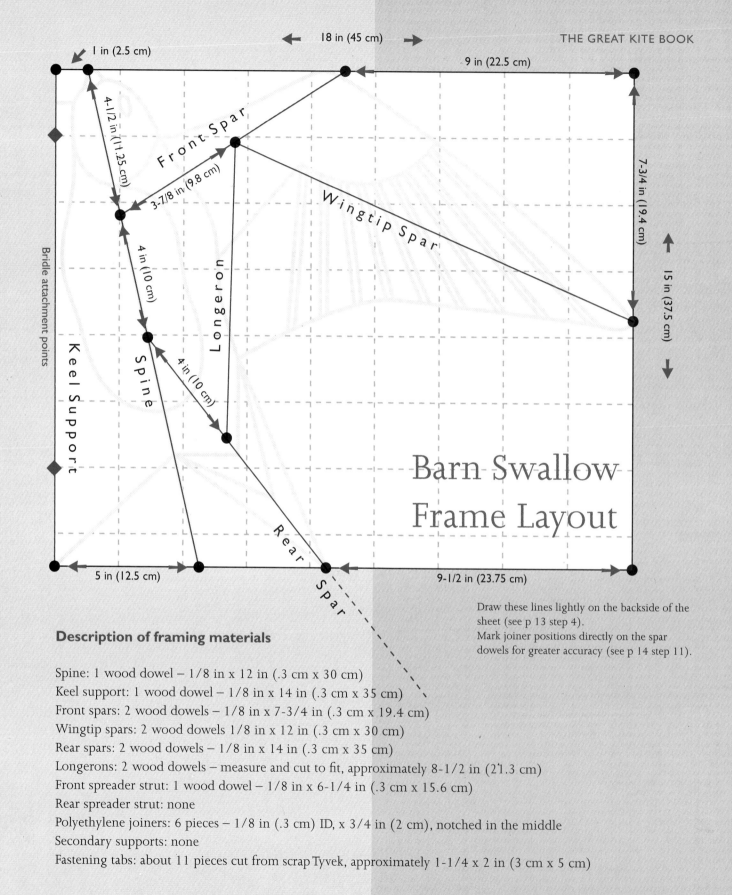

18 in (45 cm)

1 in (2.5 cm)

9 in (22.5 cm)

4-1/2 in (11.25 cm)

Front Spar

3-7/8 in (9.8 cm)

7-3/4 in (19.4 cm)

Wingtip Spar

4 in (10 cm)

Longeron

15 in (37.5 cm)

Bridle attachment points

Keel Support

4 in (10 cm)

Spine

Rear Spar

Barn Swallow
Frame Layout

5 in (12.5 cm)

9-1/2 in (23.75 cm)

Draw these lines lightly on the backside of the sheet (see p 13 step 4).
Mark joiner positions directly on the spar dowels for greater accuracy (see p 14 step 11).

Description of framing materials

Spine: 1 wood dowel – 1/8 in x 12 in (.3 cm x 30 cm)

Keel support: 1 wood dowel – 1/8 in x 14 in (.3 cm x 35 cm)

Front spars: 2 wood dowels – 1/8 in x 7-3/4 in (.3 cm x 19.4 cm)

Wingtip spars: 2 wood dowels 1/8 in x 12 in (.3 cm x 30 cm)

Rear spars: 2 wood dowels – 1/8 in x 14 in (.3 cm x 35 cm)

Longerons: 2 wood dowels – measure and cut to fit, approximately 8-1/2 in (21.3 cm)

Front spreader strut: 1 wood dowel – 1/8 in x 6-1/4 in (.3 cm x 15.6 cm)

Rear spreader strut: none

Polyethylene joiners: 6 pieces – 1/8 in (.3 cm) ID, x 3/4 in (2 cm), notched in the middle

Secondary supports: none

Fastening tabs: about 11 pieces cut from scrap Tyvek, approximately 1-1/4 x 2 in (3 cm x 5 cm)

and leaf patterns. Many had buzzers attached, making the kite "come alive" when airborne, thus better able to commune with the spirits. To this day between *April* and *June* — the monsoon period, when farmers have time to enjoy the fruits of their labors — they make and fly highly decorated kites known as *wau bulan* in a

Traditional Japanese and Korean kites.

CARP WINDSOCK

EDO KITE

O-DAKO KITE

KOREAN FIGHTER KITE

ROKKAKU KITE

NAGASAKI HATA KITE

Monarch

6

This kite requires a Tyvek sheet size of
36 in x 22 in (90 cm x 55 cm).

Shown here is the sheet folded in half to
18 in x 22 in (45 cm x 55 cm), displaying the
righthand side of the kite's face pattern. A 2 inch
(5 cm) grid is used to facilitate in transferring the
pattern onto the Tyvek sheet (see p 12).

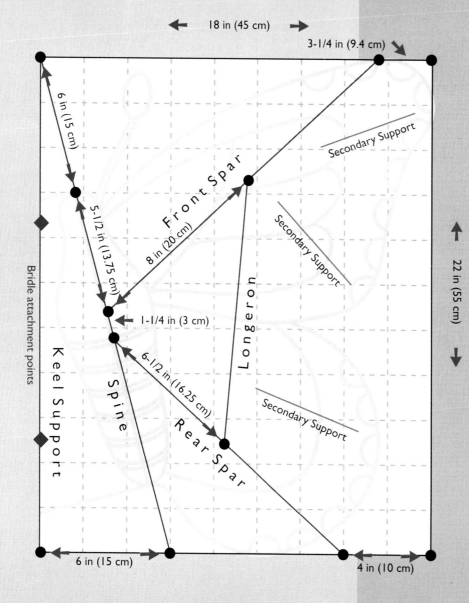

18 in (45 cm)

3-1/4 in (9.4 cm)

6 in (15 cm)

Secondary Support

Front Spar

Secondary Support

8 in (20 cm)

5-1/2 in (13.75 cm)

22 in (55 cm)

1-1/4 in (3 cm)

Longeron

Bridle attachment points

6-1/2 in (16.25 cm)

Keel Support

Spine

Rear Spar

Secondary Support

6 in (15 cm)

4 in (10 cm)

Monarch Frame Layout

Draw these lines lightly on the backside of the sheet (see p 13 step 4).
Mark joiner positions directly on the spar dowels for greater accuracy (see p 14 step 11).

Description of framing materials

Spine: 1 wood dowel – 1/8 in x 13-1/2 in (.3 cm x 33.8 cm)

Keel support: 1 wood dowel – 1/8 in x 14 in (.3 cm x 35 cm)

Front spars: 2 wood dowels – 1/8 in x 16 in (.3 cm x 40 cm)

Wingtip spars: none

Rear spars: 2 wood dowels – 1/8 in x 13 in (.3 cm x 32.5 cm)

Longerons: 2 wood dowels – measure and cut to fit, approximately 11 in (27.5 cm)

Front spreader strut: 1 wood dowel – 1/8 in x 12-1/2 in (.3 cm x 31.3 cm)

Rear spreader strut: 1 wood dowel – 1/8 in x 6-1/2 in (.3 cm x 16.3 cm)

Polyethylene joiners: 8 pieces – 1/8 in (.3 cm) ID, x 3/4 in (2 cm), notched in the middle

Secondary supports: 1/8 in wood dowels – 6 short pieces

Fastening tabs: about 15 pieces cut from scrap Tyvek, approximately 1-1/4 x 2 in (3 cm x 5 cm)

fertility ritual, not unlike the one practiced in Japan. The kites even bear similar features. It is entirely possible that they have a common origin, now lost in antiquity.

In ancient Polynesia kites were considered a gift from the gods and used to help catch fish. A length of line, tipped with a bone fishing hook, was suspended from the tail of a leaf supported by a light frame of twigs. Letting this kite fly over the water gave the fishermen on the banks a greater fishing range. Besides this practical use, kites were also used for sport in competitive community games.

In ancient New Zealand, Maori had manu (bird) kites that were half human, half bird, in shape. Birds in their culture were messengers of the gods, and such kites were used in divination ceremonies and also flown as an act of good will.

Indonesian Hindus on the island of Bali flew kites in honor of the gods Vishnu and Siva. According to legend, these gods helped rid the land of an evil king.

In Thailand the month of March is the time for the annual kite tournament. Kite "fighting" dates back to the time of King Rammi II (1809–1892). He would fly a large human-shaped kite, known as a chula (male), on the palace grounds. For sport, he allowed his courtiers to fly smaller diamond-shaped kites, called pakpao (female), which he then attempted to snag with his larger kite. The game was declared a national sport in 1921, allowing both royalty and commoners to enter teams.

In today's version the large chula is equipped with three sets of large barbs and the small pakpao with a large loop of string dangling beneath it. To play the game, a line is drawn on the ground, to divide the field into two sections. The chula is launched across this divide to where a large number of pakpaos

Shooting stars

General Gim Yu-Sin, was sent by Queen Zindong of Korea to subdue an uprising led by two rebels, Bi-Dam and Yom-Zong. On the night before battle a large shooting star streaked across the sky over the heads of Gim Yu-Sin's encamped soldiers. Believing this bad omen meant that the heavenly spirits were displeased, the soldiers refused to fight the rebels. Legend holds that to appease the men the general built a large kite, attached a giant fireworks fireball to it, and sent it aloft on the night breeze, thus symbolically returning the bad omen to the heavens. The next day the battle was fought and won.

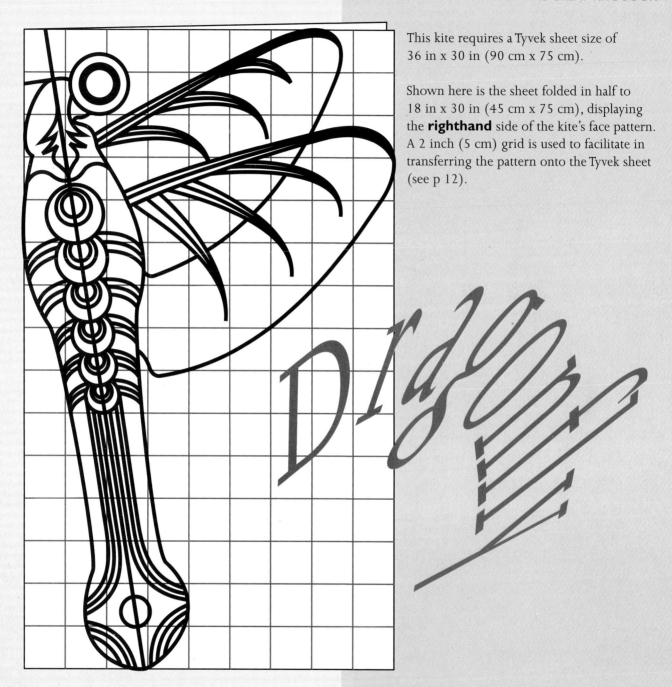

This kite requires a Tyvek sheet size of
36 in x 30 in (90 cm x 75 cm).

Shown here is the sheet folded in half to
18 in x 30 in (45 cm x 75 cm), displaying
the **righthand** side of the kite's face pattern.
A 2 inch (5 cm) grid is used to facilitate in
transferring the pattern onto the Tyvek sheet
(see p 12).

7

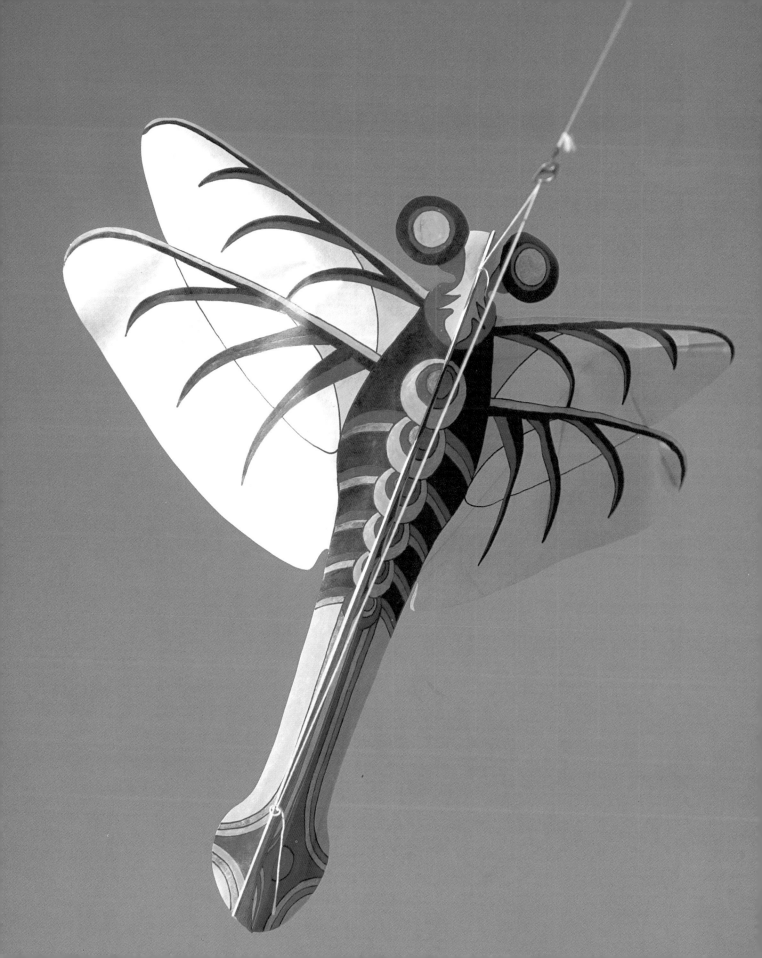

Dragonfly Frame Layout

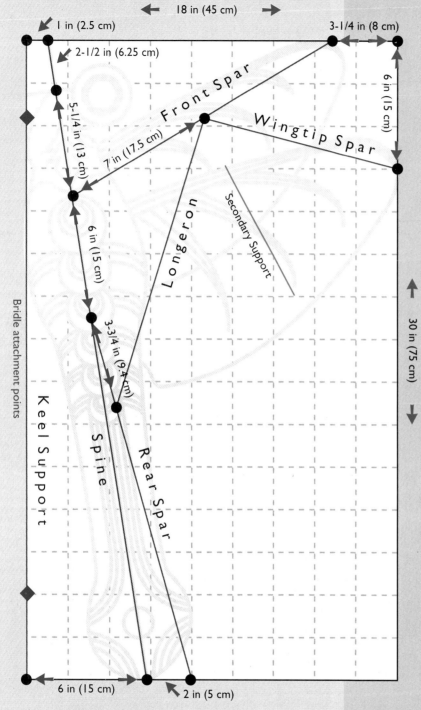

18 in (45 cm)
1 in (2.5 cm)
3-1/4 in (8 cm)
2-1/2 in (6.25 cm)
6 in (15 cm)
5-1/4 in (13 cm)
Front Spar
Wingtip Spar
7 in (17.5 cm)
Longeron
Secondary Support
6 in (15 cm)
30 in (75 cm)
3-3/4 in (9.4 cm)
Bridle attachment points
Keel Support
Spine
Rear Spar
6 in (15 cm)
2 in (5 cm)

Draw these lines lightly on the backside of the sheet (see p 13 step 4).
Mark joiner positions directly on the spar dowels for greater accuracy (see p 14 step 11).

Description of framing materials

Spine: 1 wood dowel –
   1/8 in x 28 in (.3 cm x 70 cm)
Keel support: 1 wood dowel –
   1/8 in x 28 in (.3 cm x 70 cm)
Front spars: 2 wood dowels –
   1/8 in x 14 in (.3 cm x 35 cm)
Wingtip spars: 2 wood dowels –
   1/8 in x 9 in (.3 cm x 22.5 cm)
Rear spars: 2 wood dowels –
   1/8 in x 14 in (.3 cm x 35 cm)
Longerons: 2 wood dowels –
   measure and cut to fit,
   approximately 14 in (35 cm)
Front spreader strut: 1 wood dowel –
   1/8 in x 11-3/4 in (.3 cm x 29 cm)
Rear spreader strut: none
Polyethylene joiners: 8 pieces –
   1/8 in (.3 cm) ID, x 3/4 in (2 cm),
   notched in the middle
Secondary supports:
   1/8 in wood dowels – 2 short pieces
Fastening tabs:
   about 20 pieces cut from scrap Tyvek,
   approximately 1-1/4 x 2 in (3 cm x 5 cm)

are already airborne. There are five pakpaos to each chula. The object of the game is to abduct a pakpao and drag her back across the line. The agile pakpaos, on the other hand, attempt to ensnare the cumbersome chula in their loops. It is an exciting action game, drawing large crowds of spectators.

Traditional Malay, Thai, Indian, and South Sea Island kites.

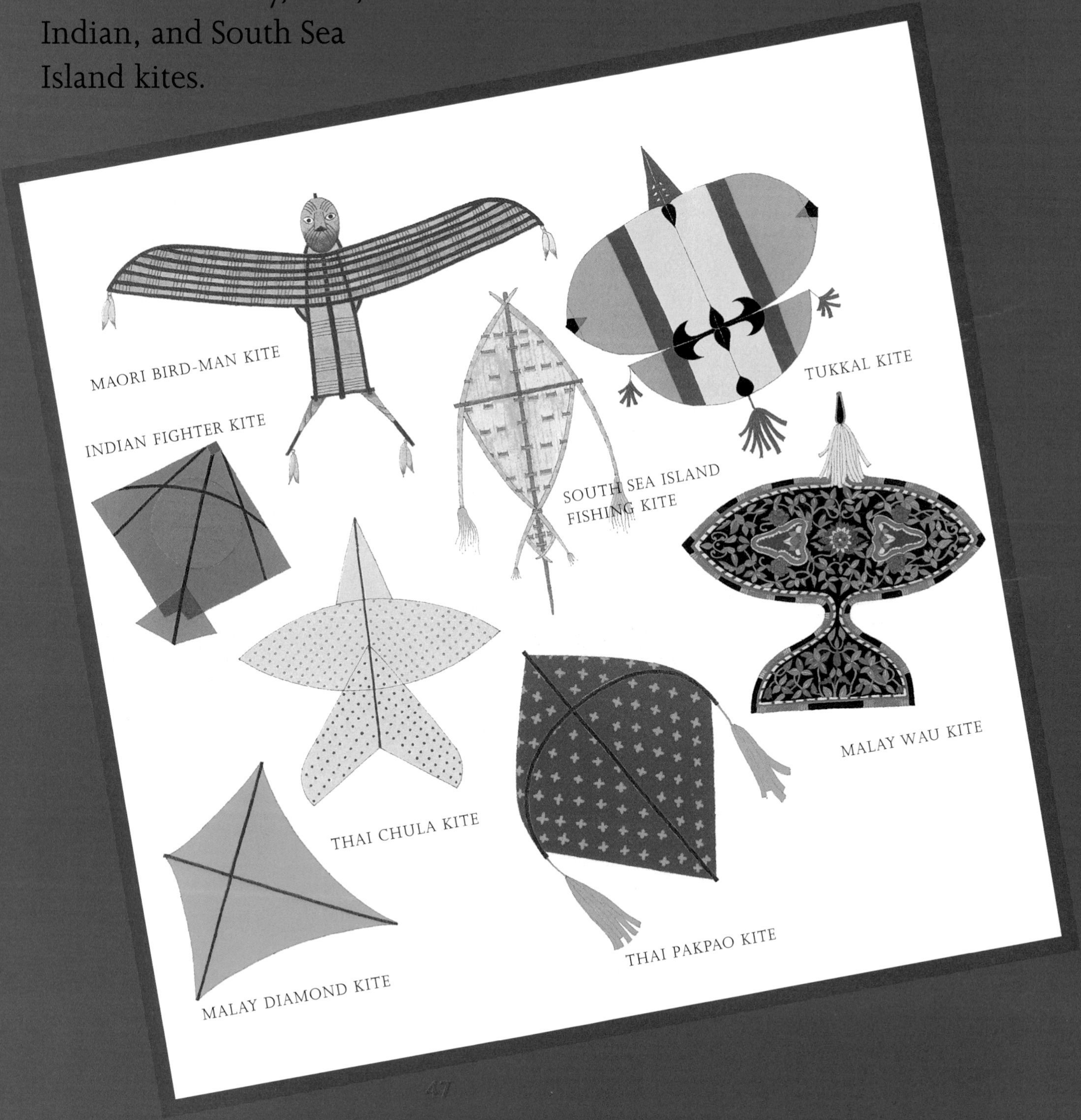

MAORI BIRD-MAN KITE

INDIAN FIGHTER KITE

SOUTH SEA ISLAND FISHING KITE

TUKKAL KITE

MALAY WAU KITE

THAI CHULA KITE

THAI PAKPAO KITE

MALAY DIAMOND KITE

8

This kite requires a Tyvek sheet size of
36 in x 15 in (90 cm x 37.5 cm).

Shown here is the sheet folded in half to
18 in x 15 in (45 cm x 37.5 cm), displaying the
righthand side of the kite's face pattern. A 2 inch
(5 cm) grid is used to facilitate in transferring the
pattern onto the Tyvek sheet (see p 12).

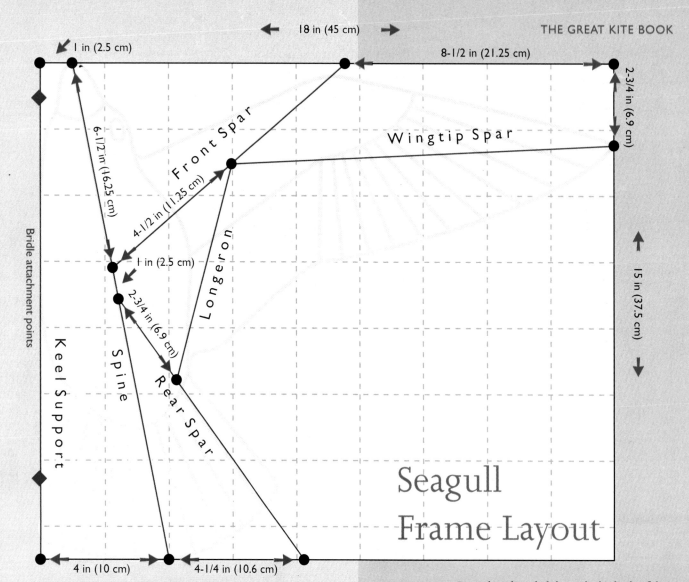

18 in (45 cm)

1 in (2.5 cm)

8-1/2 in (21.25 cm)

2-3/4 in (6.9 cm)

6-1/2 in (16.25 cm)

Front Spar

Wingtip Spar

4-1/2 in (11.25 cm)

1 in (2.5 cm)

Longeron

2-3/4 in (6.9 cm)

15 in (37.5 cm)

Bridle attachment points

Keel Support

Spine

Rear Spar

Seagull
Frame Layout

4 in (10 cm)

4-1/4 in (10.6 cm)

Draw these lines lightly on the backside of the sheet (see p 13 step 4).
Mark joiner positions directly on the spar dowels for greater accuracy (see p 14 step 11).

Description of framing materials

Spine: 1 wood dowel – 1/8 in x 15-1/2 in (.3 cm x 38.8 cm)

Keel support: 1 wood dowel – 1/8 in x 15 in (.3 cm x 37.5 cm)

Front spars: 2 wood dowels – 1/8 in x 9 in (.3 cm x 22.5 cm)

Wingtip spars: 2 wood dowels – 1/8 in x 11 in (.3 cm x 27.5 cm)

Rear spars: 2 wood dowels – 1/8 in x 7 in (.3 cm x 17.5 cm)

Longerons: 2 wood dowels – measure and cut to fit, approximately 6 in (15 cm)

Front spreader strut: 1 wood dowel – 1/8 in x 6-1/2 in (.3 cm x 16.3 cm)

Rear spreader strut: none

Polyethylene joiners: 6 pieces – 1/8 in (.3 cm) ID, x 3/4 in (2 cm), notched in the middle

Secondary supports: none

Fastening tabs: about 10 pieces cut from scrap Tyvek, approximately 1-1/4 x 2 in (3 cm x 5 cm)

In India, the winter solstice, known as Ultran is celebrated with kite "fighting." Across India the skies are awash with color as thousands of people fly kites to celebrate the end of winter. Opponents try to outmaneuver each other until one of them is in a position to cut the line of the other. During the festival, more than a million kites are purchased from local kite vendors for the purpose. Indian fighting kites are small, lightweight, and diamond-shaped, made of split bamboo and colored tissue paper. They have a small fish-tail or tassel at the tail end. Many are intricately decorated with abstract, bird, or animal patterns. To make a kite more of a threat to opponents, the upper section of the line is coated with an abrasive, consisting of a mixture of glue and ground glass.

It takes great skill to fly the skittish fighting kites and maneuver them accurately into striking position.

A farmer's misdeeds

An ancient Malaysian myth explains how a farmer and his wife found an abandoned baby girl in a field. Being childless, they took the baby home and raised her as their own. As the girl grew older she became very beautiful. The farmer was infatuated with his adopted daughter, paying her every possible attention. In her jealousy, the wife became furious and beat the girl, driving her from the farm. The young beauty was never seen again.

The farmer became despondent and his fields refused to yield crops. The couple traveled to consult a fortune-teller, to explain their misfortune. He said that because the young girl had come from the field, she had now become a sky spirit of the rice fields, and was preventing a harvest because of the farmer's misdeeds. By constructing a moon kite and flying it over the fields, the couple appeased the spirit and had an abundant harvest.

This is the basis of the annual Malaysian fertility ritual involving kites to invoke a bountiful harvest.

Hidden string

According to legend, Tan, an ancient Polynesian god, became jealous of his older brother Rango's (god of war and peace) growing prestige and challenged him to a duel with kites. Whoever could fly their kite the highest would be the winner and thus gain more power. Unknown to his brother, Rango had discovered a large quantity of string and this string allowed his kite to outfly Tan's. The two brothers remained friends and passed on the secret of making kites and competition to humans. And since ancient times kiting games have been popular in the Polynesian islands.

A kite bearing Rango's name is flown at the start of every game. The person whose kite achieves the greatest height is honored by having his kite designated as the god Rango. Rango has become the patron of kiting.

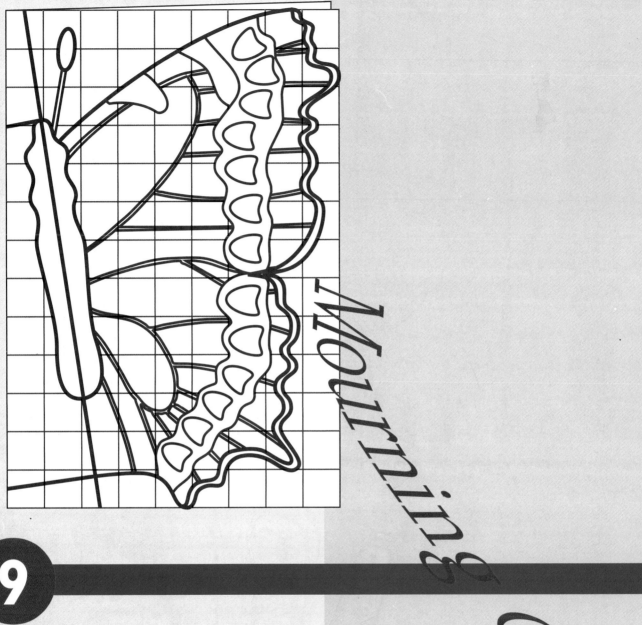

9

This kite requires a Tyvek sheet size of
36 in x 26 in (90 cm x 65 cm).

Shown here is the sheet folded in half to
18 in x 26 in (45 cm x 65 cm), displaying the
righthand side of the kite's face pattern. A 2 inch
(5 cm) grid is used to facilitate in transferring the
pattern onto the Tyvek sheet (see p 12).

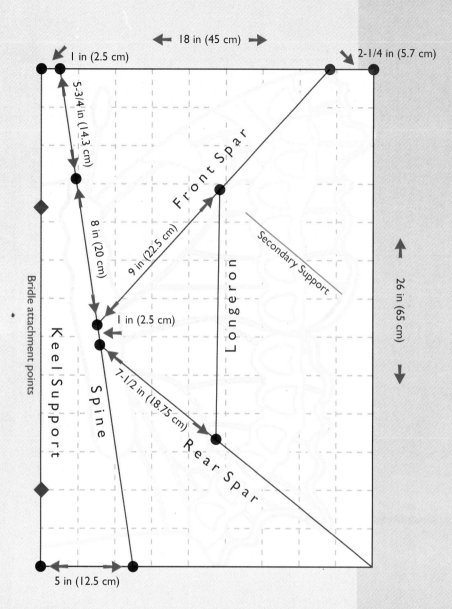

18 in (45 cm)

1 in (2.5 cm)

2-1/4 in (5.7 cm)

5-3/4 in (14.3 cm)

Front Spar

8 in (20 cm)

9 in (22.5 cm)

Secondary Support

1 in (2.5 cm)

Longeron

26 in (65 cm)

Bridle attachment points

Keel Support

Spine

7-1/2 in (18.75 cm)

Rear Spar

5 in (12.5 cm)

Mourning Cloak Frame Layout

Draw these lines lightly on the backside of the sheet (see p 13 step 4).
Mark joiner positions directly on the spar dowels for greater accuracy (see p 14 step 11).

Description of framing materials

Spine: 1 wood dowel – 1/8 in x 18-3/4 in (.3 cm x 46.9 cm)

Keel support: 1 wood dowel – 1/8 in x 18-3/4 in (.3 cm x 46.9 cm)

Front spars: 2 wood dowels – 3/16 in x 18 in (.45 cm x 45 cm)·

Wingtip spars: none

Rear spars: 2 wood dowels – 3/16 in x 15 in (.45 cm x 37.5 cm)

Longerons: 2 wood dowels – measure and cut to fit, approximately 11-3/4 in (29.4 cm)

Front spreader strut: 1 wood dowel – 3/16 in x 12-3/4 in (.45 cm x 31.9 cm)

Rear spreader strut: 1 wood dowel – 3/16 in x 8-1/2 in (.45 cm x 21.3 cm)

Polyethylene joiners: 8 pieces – 3/16 in (.45 cm) ID, x 1 in (2.5 cm), notched in the middle

Secondary supports: 1/8 in wood dowels – 2 short pieces

Fastening tabs: about 10 pieces cut from scrap Tyvek, approximately 1-1/2 x 3 in (3.8 cm x 7.5 cm)

The shepherd and the goose feather

In Bali, the myth of the shepherd and the goose feather explains how kites came into being. A ruthless king kept everyone in poverty. One poor shepherd daydreamed of better times — of meeting and marrying a beautiful young woman and living with her in a splendid house. He even drew her imagined likeness on every occasion.

The king saw the shepherd's drawings, thought it was a real woman, and became jealous and wanted her for himself. He demanded the shepherd bring her to him, on pain of death. In fright the shepherd fled into the forest where a large and fierce monster lived. The monster wished to help the shepherd. Plucking a feather from the neck of a pure white goose, he gave it a puff of his breath and it was caught up on the wind. The monster commanded the shepherd to follow the feather wherever it led.

When the feather finally stopped the shepherd heard singing, then he saw a swirl of divas (spirits) led by the god Siva (destroyer). He was awestruck. The god told him that he had met every requirement of a great test of trust, and as a reward gave him not only the most beautiful diva to be his bride, but also crowned him king of the land. Siva also explained the shepherd's daydreams to him — he was no ordinary shepherd, but was a descendent of the god Vishnu (renewer). The monster, who was an agent of the gods, killed the evil king. In honor of their new king and queen, the people flew kites shaped like a goose feather.

Kite battles are undertaken in good humor. Lost kites are seen as sacrifices to Surya the sun god. At night small paper lanterns are lofted into the sky by tukkal kites in the god's honor.

Traders plying the world's oceans during the seventeenth to nineteenth centuries probably brought kites to the Caribbean Islands and the Americas. Central American natives flew large hexagonal and octagonal kites, sun kites, at festivals in honor of the sun, an important focus in their ancient cultures. Kites in the shape of birds and other creatures were also made. Traditionally, they often sported decorative banners and noise makers.

While the global traders also brought kites to Europe, kites appear to have been invented independently in the western world. In ancient times, the Greek philosopher and mathematician Archylas of Tarentum, conducted aerial experiments with lightweight wood birds, although it is not known if this was a kite. Roman legions flew dragon-shaped cloth windsocks atop long poles. These airborne shapes connected wind and spirits and became powerful symbols of strength, evil, and destruction. Besides having the practical use of indicating to the bowmen the direction and strength of the wind, they seemed to writhe in the wind and served to inspire awe and terror in the enemy. A battlefield seemingly alive with billowing and writhing dragons had a remarkable effect on enemy morale. But real evidence of aeronautical invention occurred only after the Roman period.

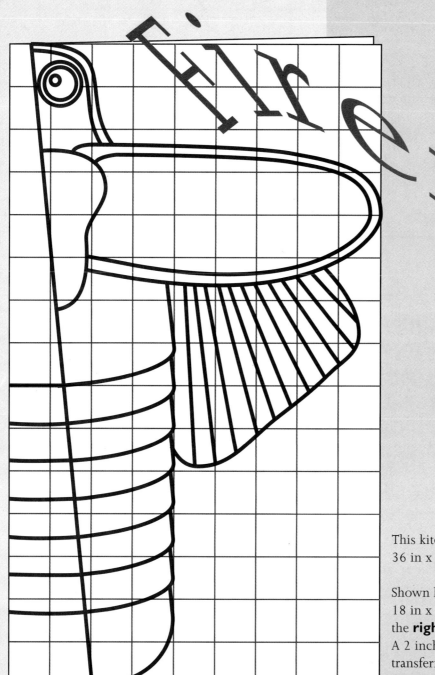

This kite requires a Tyvek sheet size of 36 in x 30 in (90 cm x 75 cm).

Shown here is the sheet folded in half to 18 in x 30 in (45 cm x 75 cm), displaying the **righthand** side of the kite's face pattern. A 2 inch (5 cm) grid is used to facilitate in transferring the pattern onto the Tyvek sheet (see p 12).

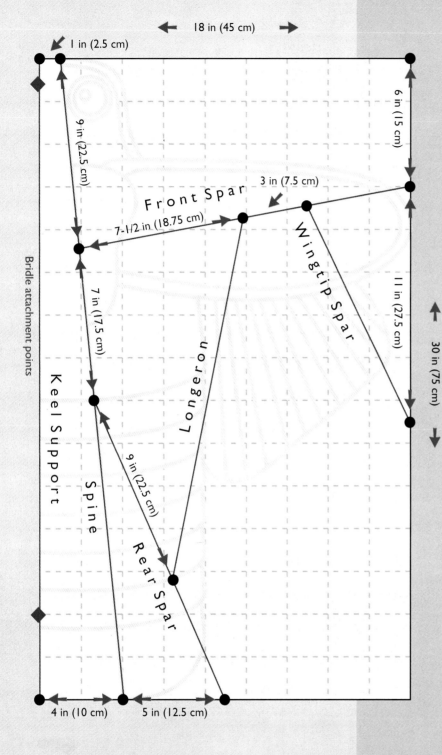

18 in (45 cm)

1 in (2.5 cm)

6 in (15 cm)

9 in (22.5 cm)

Front Spar

3 in (7.5 cm)

7-1/2 in (18.75 cm)

Wingtip Spar

11 in (27.5 cm)

Bridle attachment points

7 in (17.5 cm)

Longeron

30 in (75 cm)

Keel Support

Spine

9 in (22.5 cm)

Rear Spar

4 in (10 cm)

5 in (12.5 cm)

Firefly Frame Layout

Draw these lines lightly on the backside of the sheet (see p 13 step 4).
Mark joiner positions directly on the spar dowels for greater accuracy (see p 14 step 11).

Description of framing materials

Spine: 1 wood dowel –
  3/16 in x 30 in (.45 cm x 75 cm)
Keel support: 1 wood dowel –
  1/8 in x 30 in (.3 cm x 75 cm)
Front spars: 2 wood dowels –
  3/16 in x 15 in (.45 cm x 37.5 cm)
Wingtip spars: 2 wood dowels –
  3/16 in x 8 in (.45 cm x 20 cm)
Rear spars: 2 wood dowels –
  3/16 in x 12 in (.45 cm x 30 cm)
Longerons: 2 wood dowels –
  measure and cut to fit,
  approximately 16-1/2 in (41.3 cm)
Front spreader strut: 1 wood dowel –
  3/16 in x 12-1/2 in (.45 cm x 31.3 cm)
Rear spreader strut: none
Polyethylene joiners: 8 pieces –
  3/16 in (.45 cm) ID, x 1 in (2.5 cm),
  notched in the middle
Secondary supports: none
Fastening tabs:
  about 11 pieces cut from scrap Tyvek,
  approximately 1-1/2 x 3 in
  (3.8 cm x 7.5 cm)

Dragon windsocks were first flown freely on lines, known as draco kites. Then, to improve their performance, they were flattened out and made serpentine-like with a broad sail — pennons. Later their symbolic strength became real. By 1326 a pennon kite had been used by soldiers to bomb a fortress from the air.

Early European kites.

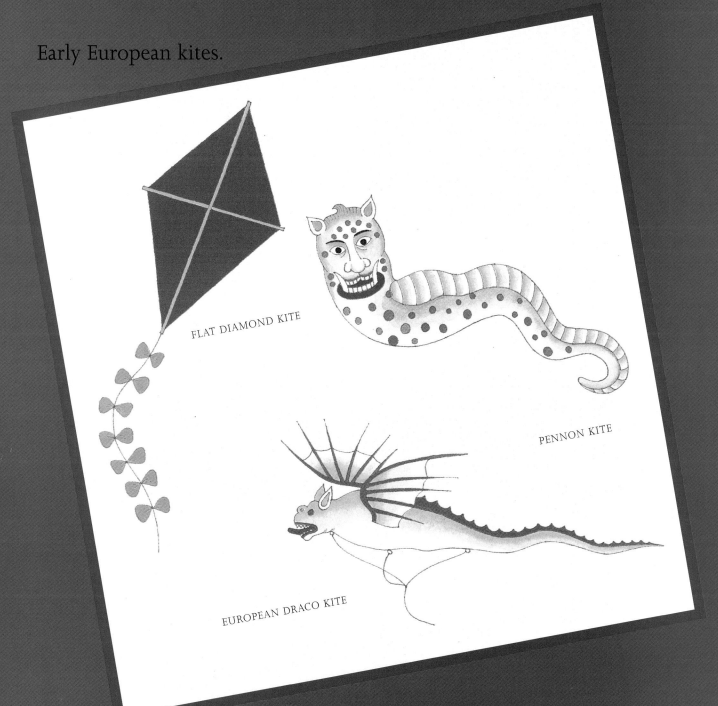

FLAT DIAMOND KITE

PENNON KITE

EUROPEAN DRACO KITE

Falcon

This kite requires a Tyvek sheet size of
36 in x 18 in (90 cm x 45 cm).

Shown here is the sheet folded in half to
18 in x 18 in (45 cm x 45 cm), displaying the
righthand side of the kite's face pattern. A 2 inch
(5 cm) grid is used to facilitate in transferring the
pattern onto the Tyvek sheet (see p 12).

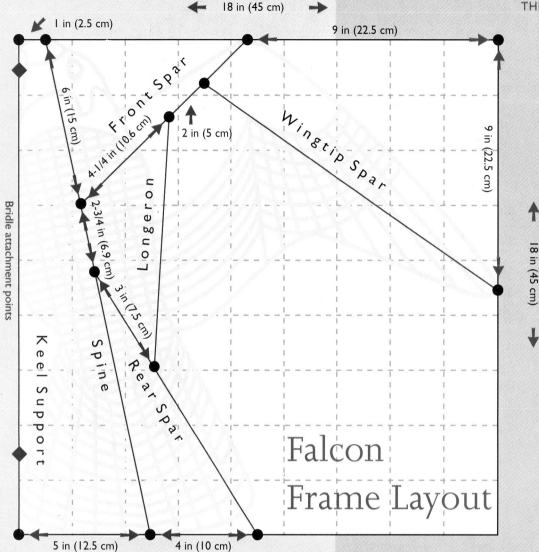

18 in (45 cm)

1 in (2.5 cm)

9 in (22.5 cm)

Front Spar

6 in (15 cm)

2 in (5 cm)

Wingtip Spar

4-1/4 in (10.6 cm)

Longeron

9 in (22.5 cm)

2-3/4 in (6.9 cm)

18 in (45 cm)

3 in (7.5 cm)

Bridle attachment points

Keel Support

Spine

Rear Spar

Falcon
Frame Layout

5 in (12.5 cm)

4 in (10 cm)

Draw these lines lightly on the backside of the sheet (see p 13 step 4).
Mark joiner positions directly on the spar dowels for greater accuracy (see p 14 step 11).

Description of framing materials

Spine: 1 wood dowel – 1/8 in x 18-1/2 in (.3 cm x 46.3 cm)

Keel support: 1 wood dowel – 1/8 in x 18 in (.3 cm x 45 cm)

Front spars: 2 wood dowels – 1/8 in x 8-1/2 in (.3 cm x 21.3 cm)

Wingtip spars: 2 wood dowels – 1/8 in x 13 in (.3 cm x 32.5 cm)

Rear spars: 2 wood dowels – 1/8 in x 10 in (.3 cm x 25 cm)

Longerons: 2 wood dowels – measure and cut to fit, approximately 8 in (20 cm)

Front spreader strut: 1 wood dowel – 1/8 in x 6-1/4 in (.3 cm x 15.6 cm)

Rear spreader strut: 1 wood dowel – none

Polyethylene joiners: 6 pieces – 1/8 in (.3 cm) ID, x 3/4 in (2 cm), notched in the middle

Secondary supports: none

Fastening tabs: about 11 pieces cut from scrap Tyvek, approximately 1-1/4 x 2 in (3 cm x 5 cm)

In Europe kites were made of heavy cloth and wood construction and not especially airworthy. Paper had yet to be made there and bamboo was unknown. Kites did not find widespread use until the advantages of lightweight construction, introduced from the Orient, were understood.

Kites and inventors

Two versions of kites, both flexible and light — the archtop "fighters" and the Malay diamond — were the first oriental styles introduced into Europe by Marco Polo towards the end of the thirteenth century. Children were attracted to them, but kites had no cultural meaning and little practical value for westerners. Builders had no understanding of kite aerodynamics and little interest in studying it, therefore these styles soon lost much of their delicacy and airworthiness. The flat diamond with a long tail of bows seen in old picture books — not a very good flyer — became the "standard kite" in Europe and America.

Kites assumed real practical value in 1749 when Alexander Wilson used them to determine the differences of air temperature at various altitudes. He was the first to fly a number of kites attached at various heights to a common line, making a "kite train." Benjamin Franklin's famous (and dangerous) electricity experiment with a handkerchief kite followed in 1752. These experiments with kites set the stage for many others to follow. By 1826 George Pocock constructed steerable kite trains with elaborate bridles and lines, using them to propel a carriage — a Char-volant. It was able to carry four or five persons up to a speed of 20 miles per hour (32 km/hr). Many stories about Pocock's adventures have been recorded, including races with kite-propelled boats.

No More Kite Lines

Between 1799 and 1809 George Cayley experimented with archtop kites. He became interested primarily in manned flight, dispensed with kite lines entirely, and concentrated on free-flight. His first craft consisted of two kites, a large one to provide lift and a smaller one for the tail, joined by a rigid frame. He experimented with control and steerage, and made calculations of how much weight various sizes of kites could lift. His work showed that lift and thrust were two different phenomena, dispelling any notion that wing flapping would get people airborne.

By 1853 Cayley had perfected his gliders sufficiently to attempt manned flight and persuaded his coachman to climb aboard his flying machine. This is the first record of manned flight of any appreciable distance.

This pioneering work with kites laid the foundation for successful powered manned flight fifty years later.

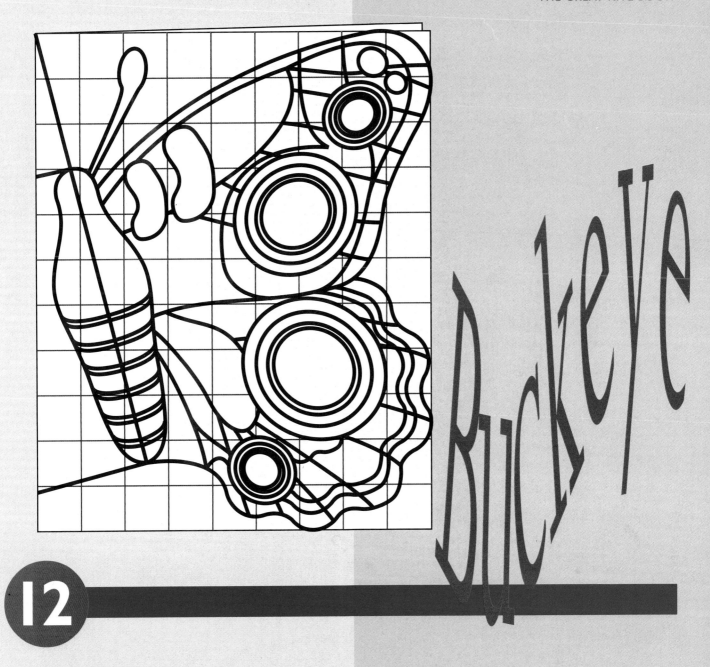

12

Buckeye

This kite requires a Tyvek sheet size of
36 in x 22 in (90 cm x 55 cm).

Shown here is the sheet folded in half to
18 in x 22 in (45 cm x 55 cm), displaying the
righthand side of the kite's face pattern. A 2 inch
(5 cm) grid is used to facilitate in transferring the
pattern onto the Tyvek sheet (see p 12).

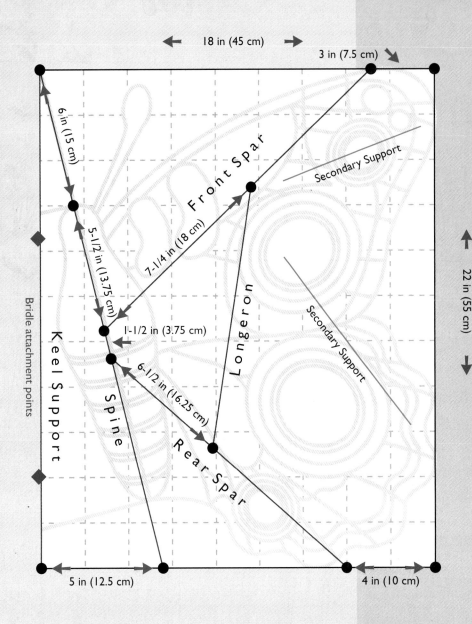

18 in (45 cm)

3 in (7.5 cm)

6 in (15 cm)

Front Spar

Secondary Support

5-1/2 in (13.75 cm)

7-1/4 in (18 cm)

22 in (55 cm)

Longeron

Secondary Support

1-1/2 in (3.75 cm)

6-1/2 in (16.25 cm)

Bridle attachment points

Keel Support

Spine

Rear Spar

5 in (12.5 cm)

4 in (10 cm)

Buckeye Frame Layout

Draw these lines lightly on the backside of the sheet (see p 13 step 4).
Mark joiner positions directly on the spar dowels for greater accuracy (see p 14 step 11).

Description of framing materials

Spine: 1 wood dowel – 1/8 in x 13-1/2 in (.3 cm x 33.8 cm)

Keel support: 1 wood dowel – 1/8 in x 14 in (.3 cm x 35 cm)

Front spars: 2 wood dowels – 1/8 in x 15-1/2 in (.3 cm x 38.8 cm)

Wingtip spars: none

Rear spars: 2 wood dowels – 1/8 in x 13 in (.3 cm x 32.5 cm)

Longerons: 2 wood dowels – measure and cut to fit, approximately 11 in (27.5 cm)

Front spreader strut: 1 wood dowel – 1/8 in x 12 in (.3 cm x 30 cm)

Rear spreader strut: 1 wood dowel – 1/8 in x 6 in (.3 cm x 15 cm)

Polyethylene joiners: 8 pieces – 1/8 in (.3 cm) ID, x 3/4 in (2 cm), notched in the middle

Secondary supports: 1/8 in wood dowels – 4 short pieces

Fastening tabs: about 12 pieces cut from scrap Tyvek, approximately 1-1/4 x 2 in (3 cm x 5 cm)

By 1847 work began on the first suspension bridge spanning the 800 foot (240 m) Niagara gorge separating Canada and the United States. Some way was needed to lay the first cable. A kite competition determined whose kite could cross the gorge and this kite carried the lines so that construction could proceed.

Kites from the "age of invention."

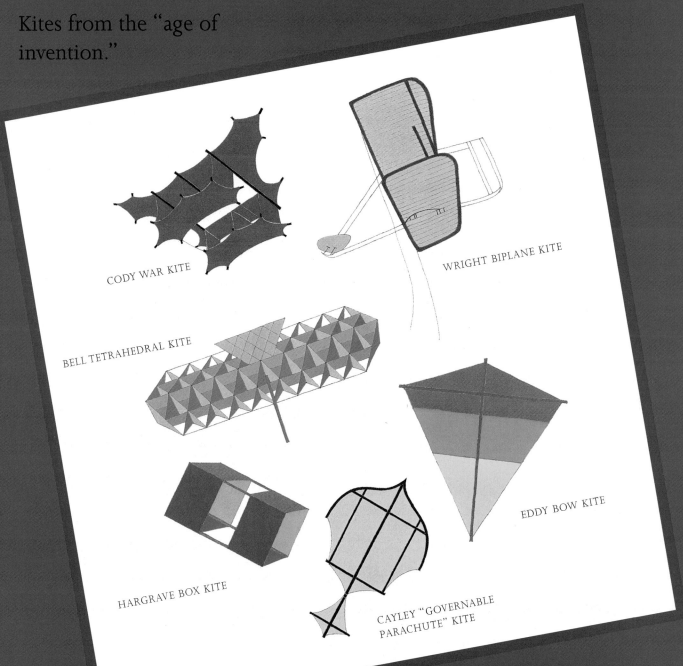

CODY WAR KITE

WRIGHT BIPLANE KITE

BELL TETRAHEDRAL KITE

EDDY BOW KITE

HARGRAVE BOX KITE

CAYLEY "GOVERNABLE PARACHUTE" KITE

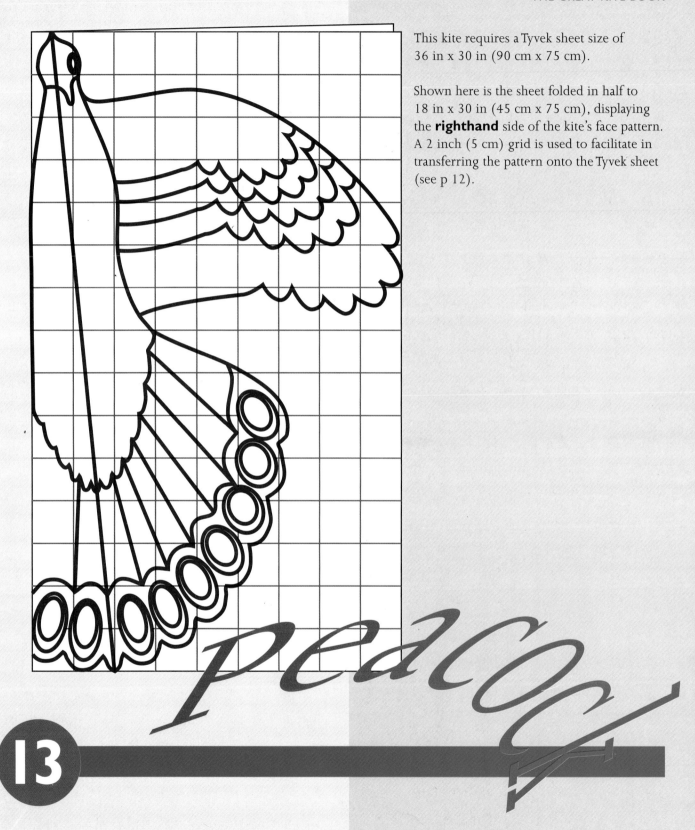

This kite requires a Tyvek sheet size of 36 in x 30 in (90 cm x 75 cm).

Shown here is the sheet folded in half to 18 in x 30 in (45 cm x 75 cm), displaying the **righthand** side of the kite's face pattern. A 2 inch (5 cm) grid is used to facilitate in transferring the pattern onto the Tyvek sheet (see p 12).

13

peacock

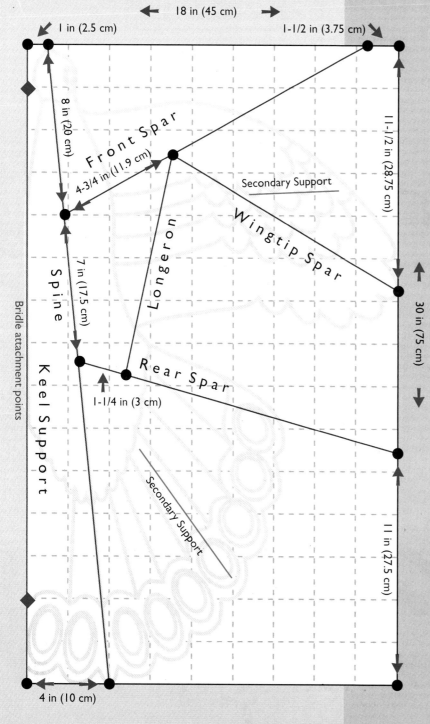

18 in (45 cm)

1 in (2.5 cm)

1-1/2 in (3.75 cm)

8 in (20 cm)

Front Spar

4-3/4 in (11.9 cm)

Secondary Support

Wingtip Spar

Longeron

7 in (17.5 cm)

Spine

Keel Support

Rear Spar

1-1/4 in (3 cm)

Secondary Support

Bridle attachment points

4 in (10 cm)

11-1/2 in (28.75 cm)

30 in (75 cm)

11 in (27.5 cm)

Peacock Frame Layout

Draw these lines lightly on the backside of the sheet (see p 13 step 4).
Mark joiner positions directly on the spar dowels for greater accuracy (see p 14 step 11).

Description of framing materials

Spine: 1 wood dowel –
  3/16 in x 30 in (.45 cm x 75 cm)
Keel support: 1 wood dowel –
  1/8 in x 29 in (.3 cm x 72.5 cm)
Front spars: 2 wood dowels –
  3/16 in x 9-1/2 in (.45 cm x 23.75 cm)
Wingtip spars: 2 wood dowels –
  1/8 in x 12-1/2 in (.3 cm x 31.25 cm)
Rear spars: 2 wood dowels –
  3/16 in x 9-1/2 in (.45 cm x 23.8 cm)
Longerons: 2 wood dowels –
  measure and cut to fit,
  approximately 9-1/2 in (23.8 cm)
Front spreader strut: 1 wood dowel –
  3/16 in x 7-3/4 in (.45 cm x 19.4 cm)
Rear spreader strut: none
Polyethylene joiners: 8 pieces –
  3/16 in (.45 cm) ID, x 1 in (2.5 cm),
  notched in the middle
Secondary supports:
  1/8 in wood dowels – 4 pieces
Fastening tabs:
  about 15 pieces cut from scrap Tyvek,
  approximately 1-1/2 x 3 in
  (3.8 cm x 7.5 cm)

Kites were again used when the United States Weather Bureau needed a reliable means of attaining upper-level atmospheric soundings. At first William Eddy experimented with large hexagonal kites in trains of up to eighteen, but when this proved unmanageable because of the massive tails required to get stability, he created a tailless kite that became known as the Eddy Bow Kite. He attained stability by bowing the spar to form a dihedral angle and using a looser covering so that the cloth billowed inward between the outer frame and the spine, forming a keel. When Eddy finally got to see a Malaysian tailless kite at the Columbian Exposition of 1893, he found that he had worked out similar aerodynamics. In 1900 he patented his kite. It was used by the Weather Bureau until it was replaced by Lawrence Hargrave's box kite, that provided more lift and stability in the air.

During the last decade of the nineteenth century and the first two decades of the twentieth century kite competitions encouraged people to experiment with lift capabilities and high altitude flight. In 1919 a train of eight kites exceeded an altitude of 30,000 feet (9,000 m) and large "man-lifting" kites turned into ship-to-shore rescue devices for vessels foundering on coastal rocks. During this time getting people airborne became an obsession and kites eventually turned into airplanes. This was largely due to the aerodynamic characteristics of Lawrence Hargrave's box kite. In 1903, the American inventors Orville and Wilbur Wright, experimenting with biplane kites (derived from box kites) succeeded in sustained manned powered flight because they discovered how to stabilize and control a free-flying "kite." And they had an adequate engine. Thus the box kite became the biplane, the standard configuration of airplanes for many years.

Kites and airplanes

Australian Lawrence Hargrave discovered that a kite shaped like an open-ended box achieved great lift and stability from the double horizontal and vertical planes. He built a great number of variously shaped box kites and used them in his manned flight experiments. His "boxes" were flown less on lines as kites and increasingly as free-flying model gliders. His objective was to eventually develop a power driven airplane.

While successful manned flight eluded him, his experiments with the cellular configuration gave the world a great new kite—the stable Hargrave Box Kite.

The box kite was used as the test vehicle for continued free-flight experiments around the world, becoming the basis for the first successful manned powered flight of Orville and Wilbur Wright in 1903. The box kite eventually evolved into the biplane, which proved to be a good airframe, and continues to be used to this day.

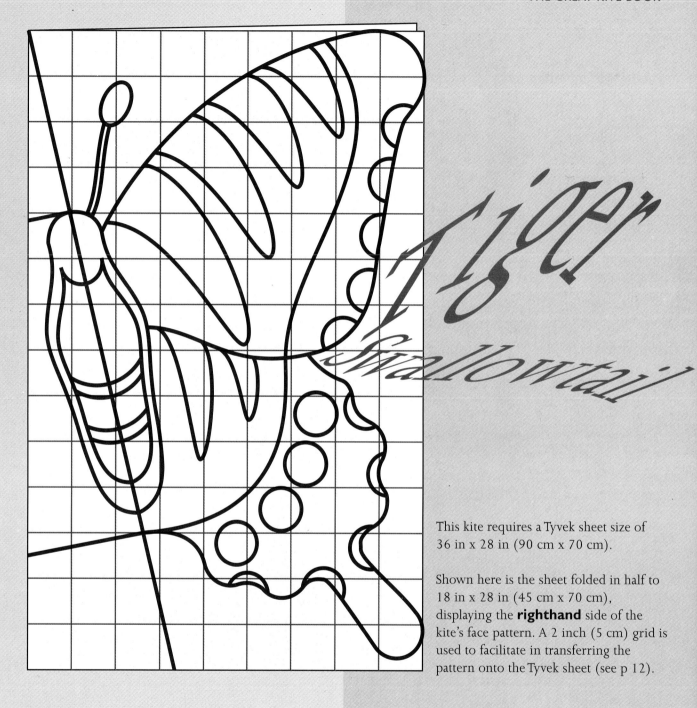

"Tiger Swallowtail"

This kite requires a Tyvek sheet size of 36 in x 28 in (90 cm x 70 cm).

Shown here is the sheet folded in half to 18 in x 28 in (45 cm x 70 cm), displaying the **righthand** side of the kite's face pattern. A 2 inch (5 cm) grid is used to facilitate in transferring the pattern onto the Tyvek sheet (see p 12).

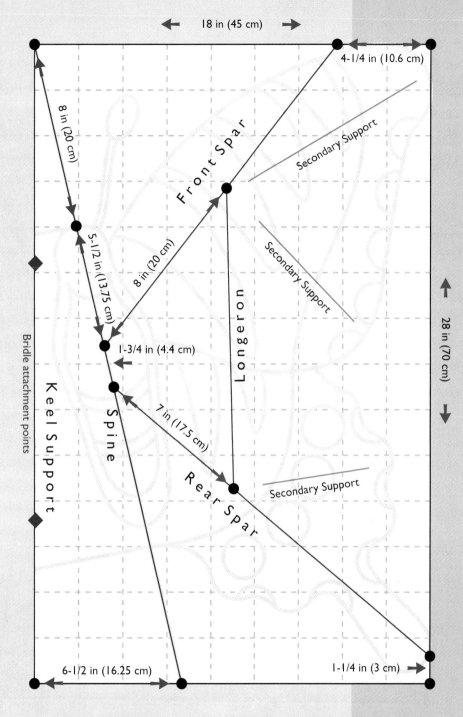

Front Spar

Secondary Support

Secondary Support

18 in (45 cm)

4-1/4 in (10.6 cm)

8 in (20 cm)

5-1/2 in (13.75 cm)

8 in (20 cm)

Longeron

1-3/4 in (4.4 cm)

28 in (70 cm)

Bridle attachment points

Keel Support

Spine

7 in (17.5 cm)

Rear Spar

Secondary Support

6-1/2 in (16.25 cm)

1-1/4 in (3 cm)

Tiger Swallowtail Frame Layout

Draw these lines lightly on the backside of the sheet (see p 13 step 4).
Mark joiner positions directly on the spar dowels for greater accuracy (see p 14 step 11).

Description of framing materials

Spine: 1 wood dowel –
   1/8 in x 14-1/2 in (.3 cm x 36.3 cm)
Keel support: 1 wood dowel –
   1/8 in x 14-1/2 in (.3 cm x 36.3 cm)
Front spars: 2 wood dowels –
   3/16 in x 16 in (.45 cm x 40 cm)
Wingtip spars: none
Rear spars: 2 wood dowels –
   3/16 in x 18 in (.45 cm x 45 cm)
Longerons: 2 wood dowels –
   measure and cut to fit,
   approximately 12 in (30 cm)
Front spreader strut: 1 wood dowel –
   3/16 in x 11-1/2 in (.45 cm x 28.75 cm)
Rear spreader strut: 1 wood dowel –
   3/16 in x 7-1/2 in (.45 cm x 18.75 cm)
Polyethylene joiners: 8 pieces –
   3/16 in (.45 cm) ID, x 1 in (2.5 cm),
   notched in the middle
Secondary supports:
   1/8 in wood dowels – 6 short pieces
Fastening tabs:
   about 12 pieces cut from scrap Tyvek,
   approximately 1-1/2 x 3 in
   (3.8 cm x 7.5 cm)

Around 1890 in England, inventor Samuel Cody increased the lift of a double-celled box kite by adding outrigger wings, making what is now called a compound kite. Besides suggesting that his kites be used in meteorological work, he proposed to use them as military observation platforms, equipping the observer

Multiline maneuverable kites.

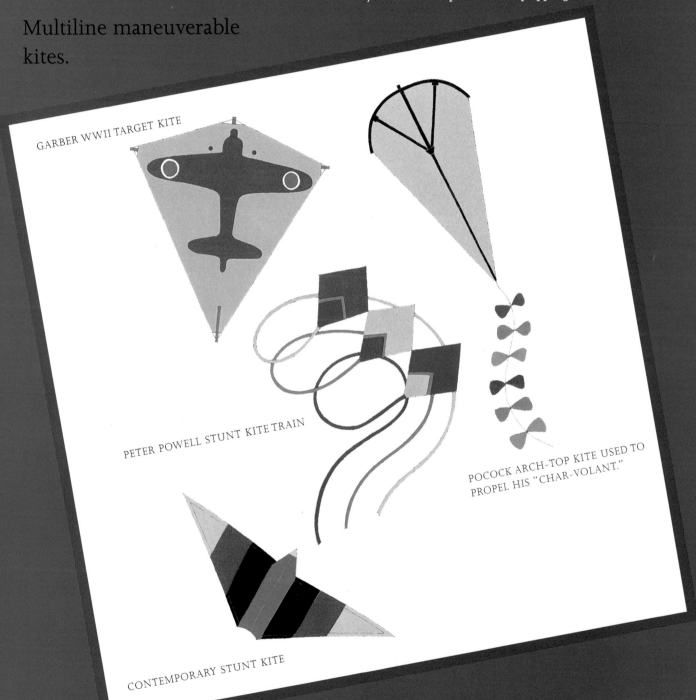

GARBER WWII TARGET KITE

PETER POWELL STUNT KITE TRAIN

POCOCK ARCH-TOP KITE USED TO PROPEL HIS "CHAR-VOLANT."

CONTEMPORARY STUNT KITE

15

This kite requires a Tyvek sheet size of
36 in x 18 in (90 cm x 45 cm).

Shown here is the sheet folded in half to
18 in x 18 in (45 cm x 45 cm), displaying the
righthand side of the kite's face pattern. A 2 inch
(5 cm) grid is used to facilitate in transferring the
pattern onto the Tyvek sheet (see p 12).

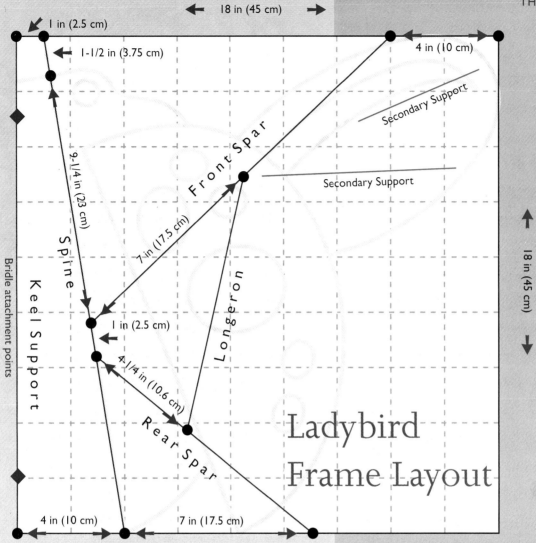

18 in (45 cm)

1 in (2.5 cm)

1-1/2 in (3.75 cm)

4 in (10 cm)

Secondary Support

Secondary Support

Front Spar

9-1/4 in (23 cm)

7 in (17.5 cm)

Spine

Keel Support

Bridle attachment points

Longeron

1 in (2.5 cm)

4-1/4 in (10.6 cm)

Rear Spar

Ladybird
Frame Layout

18 in (45 cm)

4 in (10 cm)

7 in (17.5 cm)

Draw these lines lightly on the backside of the sheet (see p 13 step 4).
Mark joiner positions directly on the spar dowels for greater accuracy (see p 14 step 11).

Description of framing materials

Spine: 1 wood dowel – 1/8 in x 17 in (.3 cm x 42.5 cm)

Keel support: 1 wood dowel – 1/8 in x 16-1/2 in (.3 cm x 41.3 cm)

Front spars: 2 wood dowels – 1/8 in x 14 in (.3 cm x 35 cm)

Wingtip spars: none

Rear spars: 2 wood dowels – 1/8 in x 8-1/2 in (.3 cm x 21.3 cm)

Longerons: 2 wood dowels – measure and cut to fit, approximately 8-1/2 in (21.3 cm)

Front spreader strut: 1 wood dowel – 1/8 in x 10-1/2 in (.3 cm x 26.3 cm)

Rear spreader strut: none

Polyethylene joiners: 6 pieces – 1/8 in (.3 cm) ID, x 3/4 in (2 cm), notched in the middle

Secondary supports: 1/8 in wood dowels – 4 pieces

Fastening tabs: about 20 pieces cut from scrap Tyvek, approximately 1-1/4 x 2 in (3 cm x 5 cm)

(who sat in a wicker basket) with a telescope, camera, telephone, and rifle. This large "man-lifter," the most famous of his kites, was known as the Cody War Kite. The British military sanctioned them in 1904. Cody continued his experiments and was the first person in Britain — as the Wrights were in the United States — to build and fly a manned powered airplane (1908), literally by putting an engine and propeller on a large kite.

Later, compound kites, called Brookites were made and distributed worldwide by Walter and Thomas Brook.

In Canada, British emigré Alexander Graham Bell, became an avid kiter. Like Hargrave, the Wrights, and Cody, he was interested in manned flight and recognized the advantages of cellular construction. Unlike them, however, he based the design of his cell unit on the tetrahedral instead of the rectangle because of its inherent triangular strength.

Taking the cell concept to the extreme, he built multicelled tetrahedral kites having as many as 3000 cells. While his celled airplanes never achieved great airworthiness because of inadequate engines, his multicelled kites were spectacular.

His interest in manned flight prompted him to form the Aerial Experiment Association, that included the American motorcycle builder and racer Glen Curtiss, specifically to develop engines for flight. A powerful engine resulted, but was never fitted to a tetrahedral craft. After this association disbanded in 1908, Curtiss, because of his knowledge of engines, went on to rival the Wrights in developing the airplane into a reliable machine.

The kite and radio

B.F.S. Baden-Powell, of the Scots Guards, realized the advantages that kites could give to the military as aerial observation platforms. But his experimental hexagonal levitor was never perfected and was never used for this purpose.

The Levitor did gain some notoriety in connection with the radio's development by Guglielmo Marconi. A Levitor kite was used to raise the radio's large aerial for Marconi's first trans-Atlantic radio transmission from Cornwall to Newfoundland in 1901. However, the kite's instability almost prevented the success of the transmission because of the aerial's erratic movement.

16

This kite requires a Tyvek sheet size of
70 in x 30 in (175 cm x 75 cm). See p 12.

Shown here is the sheet folded in half to
35 in x 30 in (87.5 cm x 75 cm), displaying the
righthand side of the kite's face pattern. A 2 inch
(5 cm) grid is used to facilitate in transferring the
pattern onto the Tyvek sheet (see p 12).

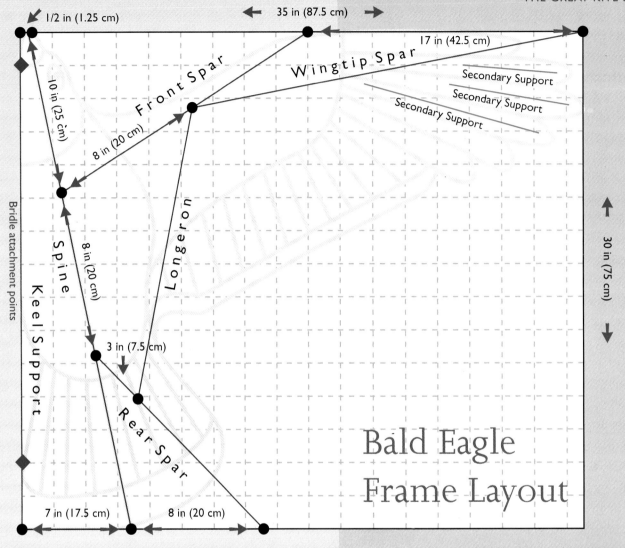

1/2 in (1.25 cm)

35 in (87.5 cm)

17 in (42.5 cm)

Front Spar

Wingtip Spar

Secondary Support

Secondary Support

Secondary Support

10 in (25 cm)

8 in (20 cm)

Spine

Longeron

Keel Support

8 in (20 cm)

30 in (75 cm)

Bridle attachment points

3 in (7.5 cm)

Rear Spar

Bald Eagle
Frame Layout

7 in (17.5 cm)

8 in (20 cm)

Draw these lines lightly on the backside of the sheet (see p 13 step 4).

Mark joiner positions directly on the spar dowels for greater accuracy (see p 14 step 11).

Description of framing materials

Spine: 1 wood dowel – 1/4 in x 30 in (.6 cm x 75 cm)

Keel support: 1 wood dowel – 1/8 in x 30 in (.3 cm x 75 cm)

Front spars: 2 wood dowels – 1/4 in x 16 in (.6 cm x 40 cm)

Wingtip spars: 2 wood dowels – 3/16 in x 22-1/2 in (.45 cm x 56.3 cm)

Rear spars: 2 wood dowels – 1/4 in x 10 in (.6 cm x 25 cm)

Longerons: 2 wood dowels – measure and cut to fit, approximately 14-3/4 in (36.9 cm)

Front spreader strut: 1 wood dowel – 1/4 in x 13-1/2 in (.6 cm x 33.8 cm)

Rear spreader strut: none

Polyethylene joiners: 6 pieces – 1/4 in (.3 cm) ID, x 3/4 in (2 cm), notched in the middle

Secondary supports: 1/8 in wood dowels – 6 pieces

Fastening tabs: about 28 pieces cut from scrap Tyvek, approximately 1-3/4 x 3 in (4.5 cm x 7.5 cm)

Between the two world wars, the kite was superseded in most scientific and practical applications by other machines and once again became an object of enjoyment for ordinary people. But, even though new kite designs were invented, the recreational use of kites was not widely pursued outside the Orient.

Twentieth-century kite innovations.

ROGALLO FLEXIBLE DELTA KITE

JALBERT PARAFOIL KITE

SCOTT/GRAUL SLED KITE

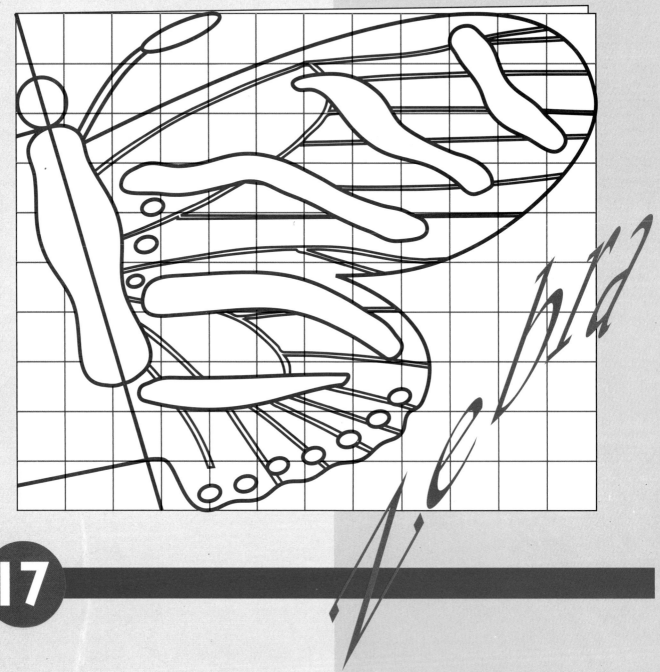

17

This kite requires a Tyvek sheet size of
48 in x 20 in (120 cm x 50 cm). See p 12.

Shown here is the sheet folded in half to
24 in x 20 in (60 cm x 50 cm), displaying the
righthand side of the kite's face pattern. A 2 inch
(5 cm) grid is used to facilitate in transferring the
pattern onto the Tyvek sheet (see p 12).

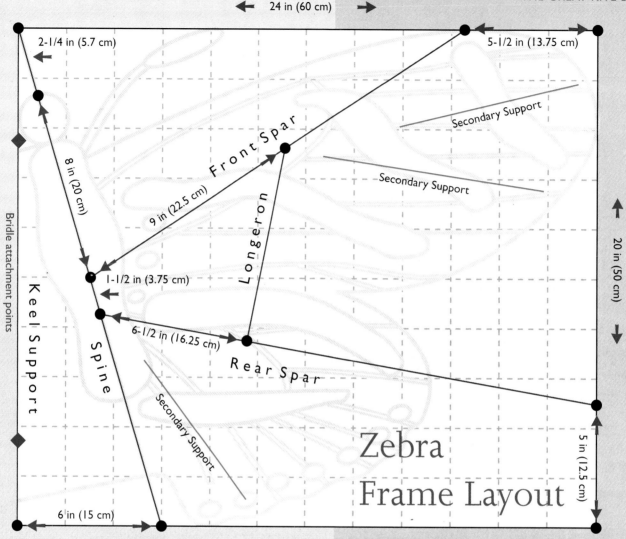

← 24 in (60 cm) →

2-1/4 in (5.7 cm)

5-1/2 in (13.75 cm)

Front Spar

Secondary Support

Secondary Support

8 in (20 cm)

9 in (22.5 cm)

Longeron

20 in (50 cm)

1-1/2 in (3.75 cm)

Bridle attachment points

Keel Support

6-1/2 in (16.25 cm)

Spine

Rear Spar

Secondary Support

Zebra
Frame Layout

5 in (12.5 cm)

6 in (15 cm)

Draw these lines lightly on the backside of the sheet (see p 13 step 4).
Mark joiner positions directly on the spar dowels for greater accuracy (see p 14 step 11).

Description of framing materials

Spine: 1 wood dowel – 3/16 in x 16 in (.45 cm x 40 cm)
Keel support: 1 wood dowel – 1/8 in x 16 in (.3 cm x 40 cm)
Front spars: 2 wood dowels – 3/16 in x 18 in (.45 cm x 45 cm)
Wingtip spars: none
Rear spars: 2 wood dowels – 3/16 in x 13 in (.45 cm x 32.5 cm)
Longerons: 2 wood dowels – measure and cut to fit, approximately 7 in (17.5 cm)
Front spreader strut: 1 wood dowel – 3/16 in x 15 in (.45 cm x 37.5 cm)
Rear spreader strut: none
Polyethylene joiners: 6 pieces – 3/16 in (.3 cm) ID, x 1 in (2.5 cm), notched in the middle
Secondary supports: 1/8 in wood dowels – 6 pieces
Fastening tabs: about 24 pieces cut from scrap Tyvek, approximately 1-1/2 x 3 in (3.8 cm x 7.5 cm)

Kites for everyone

Interestingly, long after kites had influenced airplane development and airplanes had achieved incredible advances, the airplane influenced a new development in kites. In 1948 Francis Rogallo, an American aeronautical engineer interested in spacecraft, developed a delta-shaped fabric wing having no rigid spar of any kind. It could be stowed folded into a small space when not in use, and deployed like a parachute when needed, taking shape only when the flow of air billowed it out against the counterbalancing support of numerous shroud lines. Although not used in spacecraft re-entry, the flexible delta wing (with the addition of some rigid supports) has become the favorite kite design for many enthusiasts.

Its creation also led to further experiments by others, influencing two additional developments. One was the sled kite originally developed by William Allison in the 1950s, later modified by Frank Scott and Ed Grauel. The other was the parafoil, created by Domina Jalbert in the 1960s.

During the second world war, naval officer Paul Garber introduced a technique to control kites similar to the extra lines method first used by George Pocock in 1826. He applied it to a modified Eddy Bow Kite, made with two industrial materials — an aluminum frame with a rayon sail. The kite could mimic aerial combat maneuvers and was used as a realistic target for naval gunnery practice.

Many innovations in kite design and materials in the 1970s and 80s, especially in aerobatic kites, led to increased popularity of kiting. Will Yolen promoted the art of kiting and American sculptor, Tal Streeter, who applied traditional Japanese

Kites and parachutes

Domina Jalbert realized that a conventional parachute was inefficient because it spilled a lot of air, and was dangerous because it offered limited maneuverability to the descending flier. His parafoil kite was much more buoyant because of how its multicelled configuration trapped air. He realized that it could easily be adapted for use as a parachute. It was very maneuverable because of its keel and bridle system, making controlled descents and pin-point landings possible.

This makes the parafoil ideal for military applications, enabling a pilot who has bailed out to exercise considerable evasive maneuvering. It is also widely used for controlled aerial display jumping.

Canada Goose

18

This kite requires a Tyvek sheet size of
70 in x 30 in (175 cm x 75 cm). See p 12.

Shown here is the sheet folded in half to
35 in x 30 in (87.5 cm x 75 cm), displaying the
righthand side of the kite's face pattern. A 2 inch
(5 cm) grid is used to facilitate in transferring the
pattern onto the Tyvek sheet (see p 12).

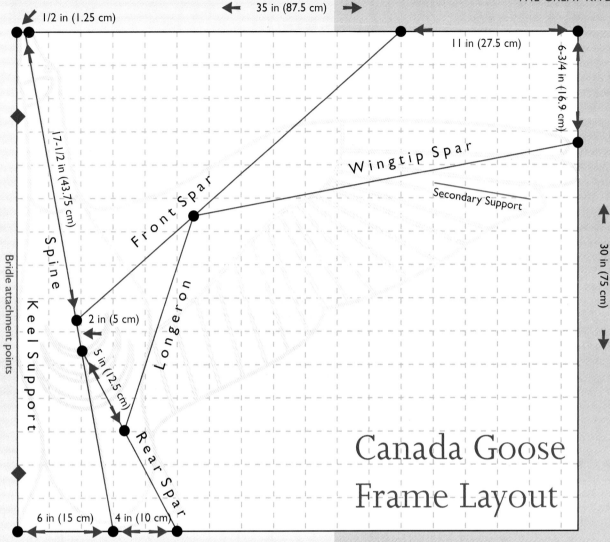

1/2 in (1.25 cm)

35 in (87.5 cm)

11 in (27.5 cm)

6-3/4 in (16.9 cm)

17-1/2 in (43.75 cm)

30 in (75 cm)

Spine

Keel Support

Bridle attachment points

Front Spar

Wingtip Spar

Secondary Support

Longeron

2 in (5 cm)

5 in (12.5 cm)

Rear Spar

6 in (15 cm)

4 in (10 cm)

Canada Goose Frame Layout

Draw these lines lightly on the backside of the sheet (see p 13 step 4).
Mark joiner positions directly on the spar dowels for greater accuracy (see p 14 step 11).

Description of framing materials

Spine: 1 wood dowel – 1/4 in x 30 in (.6 cm x 75 cm)

Keel support: 1 wood dowel – 1/8 in x 30 in (.3 cm x 75 cm)

Front spars: 2 wood dowels – 1/4 in x 17-1/2 in (.6 cm x 43.8 cm)

Wingtip spars: 2 wood dowels – 3/16 in x 24 in (.45 cm x 60 cm)

Rear spars: 2 wood dowels – 1/4 in x 10 in (.6 cm x 25 cm)

Longerons: 2 wood dowels – measure and cut to fit, approximately 13 in (32.5 cm)

Front spreader strut: 1 wood dowel – 1/4 in x 14 in (.6 cm x 35 cm)

Rear spreader strut: none

Polyethylene joiners: 6 pieces – 1/4 in (.6 cm) ID, x 1 in (2.5 cm), notched in the middle

Secondary supports: 1/8 in wood dowels – 2 pieces

Fastening tabs: about 20 pieces cut from scrap Tyvek, approximately 1-3/4 x 3 in (4.5 cm x 7.5 cm)

kite techniques to his aerial artwork, raised the kite's status in North America to objet d'art. In Japan, Dr. Toshi Ito and Hirotsugu Komura, brought scientific investigation to kite aerodynamics for its own sake. Kiting, once popular only in oriental cultures, is today providing fun and satisfaction for enthusiasts in North America, Europe, and the rest of the world.

Airborne art

American sculptor, Tal Streeter, was particularly interested in art objects that led the eye away from the object itself into the adjoining space. In the 1960s he worked primarily in metal, erecting large-scale environmental pieces. Realizing that the verticality of some of his artwork directed the viewer's gaze skyward, he became interested in placing objects in the sky itself. This led him to the world of kites, and for a number of years he lived in Japan to study traditional kite-making techniques from the old masters. His artistic expressions, once heavy and rooted in the ground, became airborne. His work reflects much of the simple beauty of the Japanese culture that inspired it. Streeter's notion of kite-as-an-art-object has done a great deal to raise the kite's status in North America.

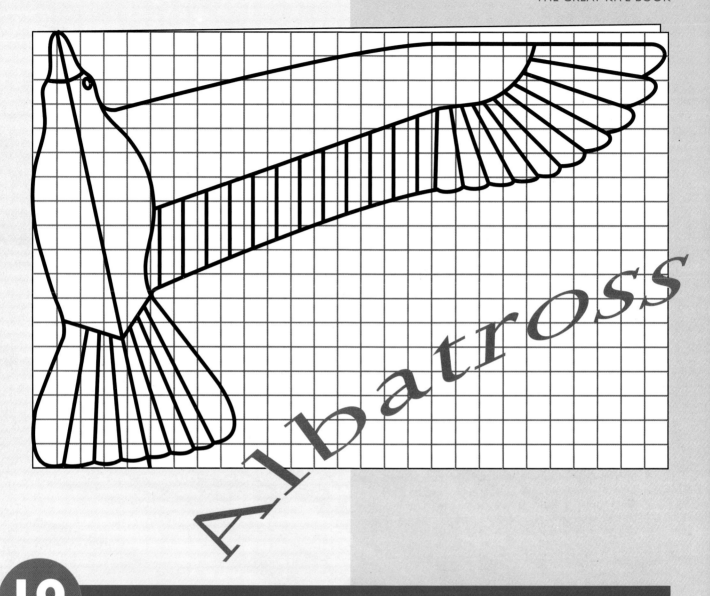

Albatross

19

This kite requires a Tyvek sheet size of 108 in x 36 in (270 cm x 90 cm). See p 12.

Shown here is the sheet folded in half to 54 in x 36 in (135 cm x 90 cm), displaying the **righthand** side of the kite's face pattern. A 2 inch (5 cm) grid is used to facilitate in transferring the pattern onto the Tyvek sheet (see p 12).

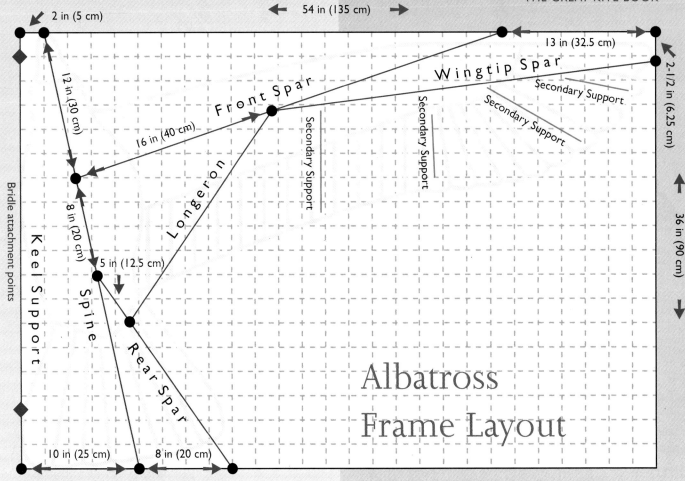

2 in (5 cm)

54 in (135 cm)

13 in (32.5 cm)

2-1/2 in (6.25 cm)

36 in (90 cm)

12 in (30 cm)

16 in (40 cm)

Front Spar

Wingtip Spar

Secondary Support

Secondary Support

Secondary Support

Secondary Support

Bridle attachment points

Keel Support

8 in (20 cm)

Longeron

Spine

5 in (12.5 cm)

Rear Spar

Albatross
Frame Layout

10 in (25 cm)

8 in (20 cm)

Draw these lines lightly on the backside of the
sheet (see p 13 step 4).
Mark joiner positions directly on the spar
dowels for greater accuracy (see p 14 step 11).

Description of framing materials

Spine: 1 wood dowel – 1/4 in x 36 in (.6 cm x 90 cm)

Keel support: 1 wood dowel – 1/4 in x 36 in (.6 cm x 90 cm)

Front spars: 2 wood dowels – 1/4 in x 32 in (.6 cm x 80 cm)

Wingtip spars: 2 wood dowels – 1/4 in x 33 in (.6 cm x 82.5 cm)

Rear spars: 2 wood dowels – 1/4 in x 17 in (.6 cm x 42.5 cm)

Longerons: 2 wood dowels – 1/4 in (.6 cm) x measure and cut to fit, approximately 20 in (50 cm)

Front spreader strut: 1 wood dowel – 1/4 in x 30-1/2 in (.6 cm x 76.3 cm)

Rear spreader strut: none

Polyethylene joiners: 6 pieces – 1/4 in (.6 cm) ID, x 1 in (2.5 cm), notched in the middle

Secondary supports: 1/8 in wood dowels – 8 pieces

Fastening tabs: about 34 pieces cut from scrap Tyvek, approximately 1-3/4 x 3 in (4.5 cm x 7.5 cm)

Glossary

Angle of attack The angle of a kite as it faces the wind, higher at the leading-edge, lower at the tail end.

Airfoil A lift-producing plane (as in an airplane wing) having a curved upper surface and a less curved lower surface, which creates a pressure differential above and beneath it.

Aspect ratio The relationship between a kite's width (span from wingtip to wingtip) and its length (chord length from front to back). A square kite has a ratio of one.

Bridle line The loop of line fastened to the spine (or keel) of a kite, to which is attached the towing ring and flying line, and is used to adjust the angle of attack.

Dihedral angle The upward slanting of the sail away from the spine to the wingtips.

Drogue A cone-shaped fabric tube fastened to the lower end of a kite's spine by a line, creating drag directly behind the kite, lending stability.

Flying line A long length of line, stored on a reel, having one end attached to a kite's towing ring, allowing the kite to rise into the air. A kite's tether.

High start A method of launching a kite where one person operates the flying line already stretched out, and another person holds the kite, releasing it into the air as the operator puts tension on the line.

Joiner A length of polyethylene tubing, notched in the middle, used to fasten wood dowels together.

Keel The vertical surface of a kite, providing yaw stability.

Longeron A framing piece that runs roughly from front to back.

Pitch Rotation around a kite's lateral axis.

Roll Rotation along the length of a kite.

Sail A kite's wind-receiving covering.

Spar A framing piece that runs roughly crosswise from the spine outward.

Spine A central framing piece that runs front to back, dividing the kite into two equal halves.

Spinner A cone-shaped fabric tube that spins, made up of a number of triangles and having numerous decorative streamers. It is fastened to the lower end of a kite's spine by a line so that the drag it creates is directly behind the kite. It stabilizes as well as decorates a kite.

Strut A framing piece that supports a kite's lefthand and righthand spars, providing a dihedral angle.

Swivel hook A fastener having a safety clasp and swivel, allowing anything attached to it to rotate freely.

Tab A small piece of material used to fasten framing pieces to the sail.

Tail A drag-creating streamer or other appendage fastened to the lower end of a kite's spine so that its drag is directly behind the kite, lending stability.

Towing point The place on the bridle where the flying line is attached to give the kite the correct angle of attack.

Towing ring The ring to which the flying line is fastened, used to adjust the angle of attack.

Wind gradient The gradual increase of the speed of the wind with increasing height from the ground up.

Wind shadow The area downwind of an object where air, having passed over the object, is turbulent.

Wingtip spar A framing piece running roughly crosswise that supports the outer section of a kite's sail.

Yaw Rotation around a kite's vertical axis.

Bibliography

Barwell, Eve, and Conrad Bailey. *How to Make and Fly Kites.* Studio Vista, London, 1972.

Evans, David. *Fishing for Angels: The Magic of Kites.* Annick, Toronto, 1991.

Hart, Clive. *Kites: An Historical Survey.* Praeger, New York, 1967.

Hart, Clive. *The Dream of Flight.* Faber, London, 1972.

Hosking, Wayne. *Kites.* Friedman/Fairfax, New York, 1994.

Ito, Dr. Toshio, and Hirotsugu Komura. *Kites: The Science and the Wonder.* Japan Publications, Inc., Tokyo, 1983.

Jue, David. *Chinese Kites.* Tuttle, Rutland, 1967.

Pelham, David. *Kites.* Penguin, Harmondsworth, 1976.

Schmidt, Norman. *Discover Aerodynamics With Paper Airplanes.* Peguis, Winnipeg, 1991.

Streeter, Tal. *The Art of Japanese Kites.* Weather Hill, New York, 1974.

Wagenvoord, James. *Flying Kites.* Collier, New York, 1969.

Yolen, Will. *The Complete Book of Kites and Kite Flying.* Simon and Schuster, New York, 1976.

Index